Becoming an
Effective
Mentoring
Leader

Becoming an
Effective
Mentoring
Leader

Proven Strategies for Building
Excellence in Your Organization

WILLIAM J. ROTHWELL, PhD
DR. PETER CHEE

New York   Chicago   San Francisco   Lisbon   London   Madrid   Mexico City
Milan   New Delhi   San Juan   Seoul   Singapore   Sydney   Toronto

1 2 3 4 5 6 7 8 9 10 QFR/QFR 1 8 7 6 5 4 3 2

ISBN   978-0-07-180570-4

MHID   0-07-180570-2

e-ISBN   978-0-07-180571-1

e-MHID   0-07-180571-0

Library of Congress Cataloging-in-Publication Data

Rothwell, William J.,
  Becoming an effective mentoring leader : proven strategies for building excellence in your organization / by William Rothwell and Peter Chee.
      p. cm.
  Includes bibliographical references.
  ISBN 978-0-07-180570-4 (alk. paper) — ISBN 0-07-180570-2 (alk. paper) 1. Mentoring in business. 2. Mentoring. I. Chee, Peter. II. Title.
  HF5385.R68 2013
  658.4'092—dc23   2012043012

*To my wife, Marcelina, and my son Froilan
and daughter Candice.*
—Dr. William J. Rothwell

To my loving mom and dad, Agnes and Thomas Chee
—Dr. Peter Chee

CONTENTS

PREFACE

The words *mentor* and *mentoring* have become veritable buzz-
words, and it's fashionable these days to utter them at just the right
moment, whether it's in front of your boss or your coworkers or fellow professionals.

But when we talk with people in private, they confess that they
are confused about the meaning of the words and some admit they
don't know how to "do" mentoring. That's rather unfortunate. That's
because mentoring, when done right, is good for the mentor, the mentee, and the mentee's organization.

This book is our response to this situation. The book opens
with an Advance Organizer that gives the reader a chance to access
the book's content quickly, making it rapidly accessible. The book is
divided into two parts. The first part is made up of the first three chapters. In Chapter 1, we explain why mentoring is in demand and what
it means for the reader personally and professionally. To mentor well,
the reader must have both the ability and the willingness. We consider
these two factors from a macro-level perspective, dealing first with
ability in Chapter 2, then with willingness in Chapter 3. We also provide a basic, no-frills definition of mentoring in Chapter 2.

In the second part of the book, we talk about the "how-to" of
mentoring. In Chapter 4, we provide the reader with a snapshot of
how a mentoring relationship should unfold. Then in Chapters 5
through 8 we deal with what we refer to as the four core skills of

mentoring: specifically, Chapter 5 addresses goal-refining; Chapter 6 reflecting; Chapter 7 modeling; and Chapter 8 storytelling. In each of these four chapters, we provide step-by-step instructions, practical advice, and illustrative stories. Chapter 9 is about closure—how to end the mentoring relationship and how to harvest the learning. Chapter 10 provides some advice on establishing a mentoring program in an organizational setting.

The book ends with several appendices and a list of selected mentoring resources.

Appendix I answers frequently asked questions (FAQs) about mentoring. Appendix II is a handout that mentors can give to mentees to clarify some basic expectations about the relationship. Appendix III provides a list of competencies for mentors and mentees. Appendix IV invites readers to rate themselves against mentor competencies. Appendix V invites readers to rate themselves against mentee competencies. Appendix VI offers suggestions on launching an effective mentoring program in an organization, and Appendix VII offers selected case studies on mentoring.

Dr. William J. Rothwell
Dr. Peter Chee

ACKNOWLEDGMENTS

William J. Rothwell would like to thank his wife, Marcelina, and his daughter Candice, for just being there for him. Although his son is stuck in the cornfields of Illinois, Froilan Perucho is not to be forgotten either for just being the wonderful person he is.

Peter Chee would like to thank his wife Eunice and his daughter Adelina for their steadfast love and support.

ADVANCE ORGANIZER
ABOUT MENTORING

Complete the following Organizer before you read the book. Use it as a diagnostic tool to help you assess what you most want to know about mentoring—and where you can find it in this book, *fast*.

The Organizer

Directions

Read each item in the Organizer. Circle *True (T)*, *Not Applicable (N/A)*, or *False (F)* in the left column opposite each item. Spend about 10 minutes on the Organizer. Be honest! Think of mentoring as you would like it to be—not what some expert says it is. When you finish, score and interpret the results using the instructions that appear at the end of the Organizer. Then be prepared to share your responses with others in your organization as a starting point for improving mentoring practices. If you would like to learn more about one of the items, refer to the number in the right column to find the chapter in this book in which the subject is discussed.

The Questions

Circle your response for each item below:	**Do you believe a mentor should:**	Chapter in the book in which the topic is covered:
T N/A F 1.	Be a leader?	1
T N/A F 2.	Be a teacher and adviser?	1
T N/A F 3.	Undertake mentoring for the personal rewards it brings to the mentor?	1
T N/A F 4.	Help new hires become integrated with the social network of a new corporate culture?	1
T N/A F 5.	Have a clear role to play despite the confusion created by management writings on the topic in recent years?	2
T N/A F 6.	Provide advice to others in areas in which the mentor is particularly good or strong?	2
T N/A F 7.	Above and beyond all else, be willing to serve as a mentor?	3
T N/A F 8.	Always have the option to say no to being a mentor?	3
T N/A F 9.	Expect the mentee to be organized for opportunities to interact, such as meetings?	3
T N/A F 10.	Expect the mentee to take initiative?	4
T N/A F 11.	Exit the relationship with the mentee when the mentee stands to gain little more from interaction?	4
T N/A F 12.	Remain flexible in the relationship with the mentee because a mentoring relationship, like life, does not follow a predefined script?	4
T N/A F 13.	Always remember that mentoring is fundamentally a personal relationship?	5
T N/A F 14.	Enjoy good interpersonal "chemistry" with those they mentor?	5

T N/A F 15.	Be able to articulate what he or she has learned from experience?	6
T N/A F 16.	Be able to "isolate" what is really useful from what he or she as a mentor has learned from experience?	6
T N/A F 17.	Teach by example—that is, by modeling?	7
T N/A F 18.	Be a good storyteller?	8
T N/A F 19.	Be able to tell compelling stories from which key learning points can be easily understood?	8
T N/A F 20.	Be able to tell stories that are Short, Entertaining, Audience-appropriate, and Learning-oriented?	8
T N/A F 21.	Be able to conclude the mentoring relationship successfully?	9
T N/A F 22.	Be able to establish a mentoring program in an organization?	10
___ Total		

Scoring and Interpreting the Organizer

Give yourself *1 point for each T* and a *0 for each F or N/A* listed. Total the points from the *T* column and place the sum in the line opposite to the word TOTAL. Then interpret your score as follows:

Score

Above 19 points	=	You may already understand key principles in effective mentoring. While improvements can be made, you have already met many of the key important requirements for a mentor.
15–18 points	=	Improvements could be made in your understanding of mentoring practices. On the whole, however, you are on the right track.
12–14 points	=	Your perceptions about the mentor's role are not as effective as they could be. Read the book and plan to make significant improvements.
Below 12 points	=	You lack understanding of the mentor's role and may not be cut out to be one.

PART I

THE FUNDAMENTALS OF MENTORING

CHAPTER 1

THE MENTORING LEADER

"If your actions inspire others to dream more, learn more, do more and become more, you are a leader."
—John Quincy Adams, Second President of the United States

"Of the best leaders, the people only know they exist; the next best they love and praise; the next they fear; and the next they revile. When they do not command the people's faith, some will lose faith in them, and then they resort to oaths! But of the best when their task is accomplished, their work done, the people all remark, 'we have done it ourselves.'"
—Lao-Tzu, Chinese philosopher, sixth century B.C.E.

The Story of Ali and Smith

We begin our book with a story, one told by our good friend, Sohail:

I know this young chap by the name of Ali. After graduating from university, he joined a management trainee program at a highly respected Asian company. There, he was placed under the tutelage, so to speak, of an expat named Smith.

Smith was an experienced, high-level executive at the company. Unfortunately, Ali found Smith to be, in his own words, "hypercritical." Pretty much everything he did "could be improved" and no compliments were forthcoming. Unsurprisingly, he called Smith a "jerk"—in private, of course. But they never confronted each other.

The situation became unbearable for Ali. He told himself that day: "Enough is enough." So he spoke with the HR people—discreetly, I should add—about his sorry state of affairs and his wish for a "mentor switch." Several days later, Ali received a call from HR. The HR person told him she would soon e-mail him a list of alternative mentors. She also pointed out that the list was generated by Smith, which Ali was disappointed to hear. His immediate reaction was "Smith probably made up this list on the fly. It's nothing more than a jerk list."

The list arrived, as promised. It contained the names of two, maybe three junior managers. Ali contacted the first name on the list—Chen—hesitantly. His fear and trepidation were, however, unfounded. Ali and Chen got along well. In fact, Ali liked Chen so much that he didn't even bother to talk to the other candidate mentors. The best part is, he learned a lot from Chen. Looking back, Ali shared this with me, "Smith's list wasn't a jerk list after all."

After two years or so, Ali felt that he had outgrown Chen's mentoring. He felt he was ready for bigger things. So he applied to join an in-house team doing a "special project." In Ali's company, if someone applied to such a thing and got accepted, he or she would automatically be considered a high potential. But Ali found out that Smith was on the selection committee and Smith was going to head the team as well. He was upset, to say the least. He was seriously thinking about withdrawing his application, but he finally decided to go through with it.

As expected, the selection process was tough. The poor boy was grilled, and Smith led the grilling. He thought he would never make the cut. But to his surprise, he did.

It wasn't the only surprise, though. Ali felt that working with Smith the second time around was different—different as in better. Smith was as tough as before, to be sure. What had changed was Ali, who felt he was more ready for Smith's tough style. Ali was ready to be pushed, and Smith pushed him hard.

Ali also changed his perception about Smith. He figured that Smith had had his best interest at heart all along.

"What's the evidence?" I asked him.

He cited the jerk list which turned out to be a great list. He also gave me another clue: He discovered that Smith had advocated for his inclusion on the special project team.

"OK, but what about all the hypercritical things that Smith said earlier?"

"Ah, that's a non-issue. Smith could have gone a bit easy on a newbie like me, to be sure. But at the same time, I wasn't ready professionally myself to handle that sort of heat back then. I can now say to him, professionally and confidently, 'Bring it on.'"

"So, would you now consider Smith as your mentor?" I inquired.

"Absolutely" was his reply. It was immediate and without any hint of reservation.

When the special project ended, the two unofficially extended their mentoring relationship. In fact, they are mentor and mentee up till today.

"Now that's a great mentoring story, wouldn't you say?" Sohail asked, somewhat rhetorically. We nodded in agreement. It wasn't a perfect mentorship, to be sure. (Nothing in this world is perfect, anyway.) Despite missteps along the way by both mentor and mentee, it's a great mentorship nonetheless because it worked in the end and is still working.

After a brief moment of silence, one of us said, "Ali's something of a decent mentee." Again, we nodded. The way Ali reframed his reality was certainly noteworthy.

Another remarked, "Don't forget Smith. Smith was great too. He was a mentoring leader."

"A mentoring leader," mused Sohail, "now that's an interesting phrase."

It's interesting indeed and most relevant to this book.

The Mentoring Leader

A mentoring leader is simply "a leader who mentors." The two key words in this definition are *mentoring* and *leader*. Let's consider the latter first.

The word *leader* can refer to anyone who directs people they are responsible for in the workplace. If you have one or more individuals reporting to you, you are a leader. And we're sure many of you are already one. Leaders influence other people.

Mentoring, on the other hand, means teaching and/or advising. It also involves what we call "uplifting behaviors"—namely inspiring, motivating, and encouraging. Its core purpose is to enable the mentee's growth. (The "mentee" is the person the mentor mentors.)

In the opening story, Smith wasn't a perfect mentor. For example, he inadvertently made life miserable for Ali. Nevertheless, he did do the important things right. He didn't take Ali's complaint personally. Although Ali was said to have interacted with HR discreetly, a veteran like Smith could tell it's a complaint—how else would one describe the premature termination of a mentoring relationship? Smith could have done something vindictive toward Ali. But he did no such thing. Instead, he provided Ali with a list of alternative mentors. These alternatives were more junior and more appropriate for a newbie like Ali. Smith was tough on the surface. But Ali looked beneath it and saw the good Smith was trying to do. Smith is without doubt a mentoring leader.

Other better-known mentoring leaders include Jack Welch, the former CEO of GE, and Lou Gerstner, the former CEO of IBM. They are better-known largely because they led huge and successful organizations.

Can you be a mentoring leader? Of course, you can. In fact, you should. Here's why: When we meet with company executives, we often hear this refrain: "We want our (positional) leaders to mentor." In other words, many of today's organizations want mentoring leaders.

If you are one, you are in demand and organizations are prepared to recognize or reward you for your effort. According to Allen, Lentz, and Day (2006), mentors tend to:

- Make more money than nonmentors.
- Get promoted more often than nonmentors.
- Enjoy greater career success than nonmentors.

Besides those three benefits, there are others as well. Ensher and Murphy (2005) have compiled one such list:

- A mentor gains satisfaction and pride in seeing mentees grow.
- A mentor wins the respect of others and enjoys "reputation enhancement."
- A mentor can learn new things from his or her mentee.
- A mentor can build a support network consisting of past and present mentees.

Many organizations are committed to mentoring. In the United Kingdom, for instance, the Chartered Institute of Personnel Development (CIPD) found in a survey that:

- 79 percent of respondents reported that they now use mentoring and coaching in their organizations.
- 61 percent of respondents reported that mentoring and coaching interventions had been effective.
- 99 percent felt that coaching and mentoring can deliver tangible benefits to both individuals and organizations.
- 92 percent agreed that when mentoring and coaching processes are managed effectively they have a positive impact on the organization's bottom line.

Mentoring at Agilent

Agilent has a Next Generation Leadership program in which mentoring figures prominently. As part of the strategic planning process, Agilent leaders consider talent requirements and plan to use mentoring to help meet those requirements. The program seeks to match talented people with senior managers as prospective mentors. Mentoring is part of the Agilent Sharing Knowledge (ASK) framework which aims to speed up an individual's "time to competence." An assumption is that knowledge sharing can help speed up the time it takes to make a worker productive.

Source: Adapted from R. Emelo, "Conversations with mentoring leaders," *T + D* (June 2011): 34.

All these benefits are sure to excite any sensible and forward-thinking individual—or leader. Use the tool appearing in Exhibit 1-1 to assess your own interest in mentoring.

Exhibit 1-1: Mentor Self-Assessment

Directions: Use this tool to assess your interest in mentoring. For each item in the left column, rate how much you agree in the right column. Use the following scale in the right column: **0 = Not applicable to me; 1 = No agreement at all; 2 = Not much agreement; 3 = Some agreement; 4 = Much agreement; 5 = Very much agreement.** Although answers are not right or wrong in any absolute sense, use the scores at the end of this self-assessment to do some self-reflection on your willingness to be a mentor.

Mentoring Characteristics	How Much Do You Agree?					
How much would you agree with each of the following statements?						
1 I would gain satisfaction from serving as a mentor.	0	1	2	3	4	5
2 I would experience pride in watching people grow while they are mentored by me.	0	1	2	3	4	5
3 I believe I would win respect by serving as a mentor.	0	1	2	3	4	5

4	I would enhance my reputation by serving as a mentor.	0	1	2	3	4	5
5	I believe I would learn new things by serving as a mentor.	0	1	2	3	4	5
6	As a mentor I would build a support network consisting of past and present mentees.	0	1	2	3	4	5
7	I believe I would probably make more money if I mentored others.	0	1	2	3	4	5
8	I believe I would be promoted more often if I mentored others.	0	1	2	3	4	5
9	I believe I would enjoy greater overall career success if I mentored others.	0	1	2	3	4	5
10	I believe that I would be successful as a mentor.	0	1	2	3	4	5
Total all numbers in the right column and insert the score in the box at right.							

Scoring

50–41   You feel motivated to be a mentor and feel the value of it.

40–31   You feel some motivation to be a mentor and realize some benefits.

30–21   You have a lukewarm attitude about being a mentor.

20–11   You don't feel much motivation to be a mentor despite the possible benefits to be gained from it.

10–0   You feel no motivation to be a mentor and probably would not be successful if you tried it out.

The question is: What is it that mentoring leaders can do for organizations? For starters, they can contribute to the following:

- Support new employees
- Identify talented employees
- Develop and retain talented employees

Let's look at each of these three contributions briefly.

Mentoring Leaders Can Support New Employees

When people join a new workplace, they want to feel welcomed, which is true for most, if not all, people. It doesn't matter whether it's their first job or their last one before retirement. On top of that, they also want to be able to hit the ground running.

Mentoring leaders can facilitate and accelerate this transition. For example, the mentor can plug the mentee into a workplace network and this human network can provide the mentee with the necessary support, information, and resources to get his or her work done. By doing so, the mentor helps to transform the outsider into an insider and the new hire into an effective contributor, all within a comparatively short period of time.

Mentoring Leaders Can Identify Talented Employees

The phrase *talented employees* can refer to people who are more productive than their coworkers and who can and want to be promoted. They can be workers who are not yet positional leaders or current positional leaders who are ready for bigger things.

If you have the right tools, you can identify productive workers easily. The second part is, however, less straightforward. For example, it's possible to have people who can be promoted but who don't want to be. On the other hand, some people are technically competent but are not good at managing other people—they cannot be promoted.

Mentoring leaders can help to solve this human-capital puzzle, because mentoring is fundamentally a relationship, which means mentors have ample opportunities to observe their mentees up close. They know what makes their mentees tick and are in a good position to assess whether they are promotion material and whether they want a promotion. In short, mentoring leaders make great talent scouts.

Mentoring Leaders Can Develop and Help Retain Talented Employees

One common reason given to explain why talented employees leave their organizations is that they feel they are "not getting enough development." When asked to define development, these employees include the things that help prepare them for a higher-level job. Hence, one of the things organizations can do to prevent a talent exodus is to develop talent continually, and mentoring is a great way to do so. Research also suggests that people who are involved in a mentoring relationship with an intra-organizational mentor are less likely to quit their current jobs (Allen, Finkelstein, and Poteet, 2009).

These three mentor-related contributions ensure that an organization's talent pipeline is sustainable. And as management writers John Hagel, John Seely Brown, and Lang Davison assert, "Talent is *everything*" (2009, emphasis added).

Other mentoring-related benefits at the organizational level include organizational attractiveness and knowledge management.

Organizational Attractiveness

Job applicants tend to find organizations with an established mentoring program more attractive than those without one (Allen and O'Brien, 2006). That's because the presence of a mentoring program signals that the organization cares about its people and wants to develop them.

Knowledge Management

Mentoring helps to retain and/or disseminate useful organizational knowledge (Murrell, Forte-Trammell, and Bing, 2009). It can be most useful in knowledge transfer efforts, an area of growing importance in talent management (Rothwell, 2011).

The Road Ahead

You've already seen how mentoring leaders can benefit organizations, mentees, and themselves. If you are already a positional leader, you may be asking the question: How do I mentor? But before you answer that question, we encourage you to seriously consider another question: Are you ready to mentor?

That question isn't as simple as it sounds. According to experts, one's readiness to mentor is a function of one's *ability* and *willingness* to mentor. If you want to be a good mentor, both factors are essential.

In the next chapter, we will look at the question of ability and consider it from a macro-level perspective. That is, we'll be dealing with the "what does a mentor do" question rather than the "how does the mentor do what he or she is supposed to do" question (i.e., the micro-level perspective). This approach is necessary because of confusion over the words *mentor* and *mentoring*, and clarification is in order.

Finally, one must address the issue of willingness: just because you can doesn't mean you want to. How can you know for sure that you want to? At the same time, in what ways can we boost our willingness? We will consider these questions in Chapter 3.

CHAPTER 2

THE JOB DESCRIPTION

"Now, there is one outstandingly important fact regarding mentoring, and that is that no job description comes with it."
—The ITD Mentoring Team
A parody of a R. Buckminster Fuller quote, with apologies

Going Back to Basics

What does a mentor do?

The answer to that question should be straightforward, but the mentoring literature has unfortunately complicated matters. Over the years, people from all walks of life have attached layers of meanings to the words *mentor* and *mentoring*. The cumulative result of these actions is confusion, with virtually no agreement on the meaning of the word. Garvey (2004) has even suggested that we will never reach consensus. Hence, defining the word seems to be something of a fool's errand. Nevertheless, define it we must, because a clear definition is required in every context; and every context includes this book. Otherwise, you wouldn't know what we mean whenever we use the word *mentor*.

Here's how we arrived at our definition. First, we peeled away the layers of meanings built up over time. To do so, we went back to the basics. "Basics" in this case meant the ordinary dictionary. Typically, a dictionary provides the most rudimentary definitions of words that are in use today; it was thus a natural ally in our effort to get rid of the layers. And since we are users of American English, we selected the authoritative *Webster's New World College Dictionary* (Fourth Edition) as our reference.

Dutifully, the dictionary provided us with two definitions:

- A "wise, loyal advisor"
- A "teacher or coach"

In sum, the mentor's job is to advise or to teach/coach.

The first part of the job description—advising—is clear-cut. The second part, however, is confusing: *Is the mentor a teacher or coach?*

In today's workplace, we tend to think of teaching as a *directive* way of helping people (i.e., it involves a lot of telling) and coaching as a *nondirective* way of helping people (i.e., it involves a lot of asking). In other words, the two are worlds apart and don't quite belong together. But Ives (2008) looked into the history of coaching and found that teaching and coaching were once upon a time closely linked—namely, coaching was in the past directive. Given the historical links, it is not so much of a surprise to see the dictionary lump the two together.

It is worth noting that, even though teachers in Asian cultures are often directive, the same is not true in Western cultures. In fact, the greatest teacher of Western culture was (arguably) Socrates. The Socratic method involved asking questions. In short, Socrates did not lecture to his students, but rather used questioning to shape their thinking and encourage them to think for themselves.

Nevertheless, experience tells us that teaching may play a more prominent role than coaching in today's mentoring. But that doesn't mean teaching and coaching are mutually exclusive; that is, it is not an either/or sort of situation. (See the Mentors and Coaches in Today's Workplace feature for a brief discussion on this issue.)

Therefore, the *tentative* definition becomes:

A mentor is an advisor or teacher.

The definition is "tentative" because we were not sure how well it reflected current workplace realities.

To check, we talked with people who were recognized as mentors. Their response was overwhelmingly affirmative: "That's what we do" (or some other synonymous remark) was the constant refrain.

We also spoke to mentees to double-check, and their responses were similarly positive. At the same time, our conversations with them revealed something extra: Great mentors do both—they advise as well as teach. And the mentees were quite unanimous and adamant about this point. In light of this finding and the fact that this book is about excellent mentoring, we thought it necessary to tweak our definition. Hence, the *final* definition is as follows:

> A *mentor is an advisor* and *teacher.*

MENTORS AND COACHES IN TODAY'S WORKPLACE

Mentors and coaches differ in a fundamental way: The mentor is focused on the mentee's growth; whereas the coach is focused on the coachee's job performance. Performance is by and large about meeting one's quarterly, biyearly, or yearly performance indicators; and coaching is about ensuring that those short-term targets are met. The coach therefore pays close attention to the specific skills, behaviors, and knowledge that the coachee currently needs or will need in the near term. Growth, on the other hand, is about development. Like performance, development can be understood as achieving certain targets. But unlike performance targets, development targets are several years out, so the growth time frame is typically a couple of years but likely longer. Development is also broader in scope and will likely include general knowledge and skills.

Mentors and coaches also differ in a big way in terms of behavior: The mentor is generally directive, whereas the coach nondirective. That is, the mentor downloads content into the mentee's head through teaching; while the coach draws content out from the coachee through questioning. This approach implies that the mentor must have the right content. In addition, the mentor downloads based on the assumption that the mentee does not have the requisite content to handle a particular situation. In contrast, the coach assumes that the coachee already has the requisite content, and all the coachee needs, then, is some help to unlock the solution within. It's important to realize that both assumptions could turn out wrong. Their validity is, in fact, primarily mentee-dependent. If the mentee doesn't know enough, then mentoring is the right way forward. If the mentee, however, has the right content in the right amounts to deal with a particular situation, then coaching is the right way forward. In the latter, the mentor adopts a nondirective style of helping; the mentor facilitates rather than dictates. The two key takeaways for the mentor are, first, don't jump to conclusions about your mentee. Take time to know him or her so that you're able to make an informed decision as to which style is more appropriate. If you're mentoring a mentee who's actually ready for coaching, you're likely to irritate them with your pedagogic style. Second, don't hesitate to use a combination of mentoring and coaching. You may even do so within a single mentoring session. It would be inadvisable to plan thusly: "This week, I am going to mentor Bob. Next week, I am going to coach Bob." What would work better is to use X percent of mentoring and Y percent of coaching with Bob whenever the two of you meet. You can learn to appreciate the fact that there is a time to mentor and a time to coach; and wisdom is knowing when to do which.

The Job Description: Part 1

Let's now consider each mentoring function or behavior in more detail.

The Mentor as Advisor

An advisor is a person who gives advice. And to advise is to recommend a course of action. To be able to do so requires wisdom, as the dictionary definition implies. Wisdom is generally associated with knowledge or experience. So the advisor must first have knowledge or experience in a particular area or areas of work. Potential areas include but are not limited to the following:

- Organizational culture: How things are done and what is expected at the mentee's organization, or how to thrive in a unique corporate culture
- The informal networks in the mentee's organization, and how the mentee can leverage them to get things done
- How to succeed in company politics
- Seeing the big picture: How all the different "pieces" fit together in an organization or industry
- How to work with people from other national cultures
- The important trends in the mentee's profession or industry, and how they may impact his or her career
- Work–life balance

In addition, the dictionary also characterizes the advisor as "loyal." Here, loyalty refers of course to loyalty to the mentee. It essentially means having the mentee's best interest at heart, without any conflict of interest between the mentor and the mentee. Loyalty, however, isn't blind. When the mentee does something illegal or unethical, the mentor will need to take appropriate action.

The Mentor as Teacher

The "subjects" that the mentor teaches the mentee are:

- General work-related knowledge and skills
- Specific work-related knowledge and skills

General knowledge and skills are the knowledge and skills *everybody* needs to get ahead in the mentee's organization (e.g., presentation skills and communication skills). Specific knowledge and skills refer to the technical/specialist knowledge and skills relevant to the mentee's *current* job. The same mentor can, of course, teach both subjects.

In the case of teaching, the dictionary does not provide any clues about the qualifications of a teacher. So we had to search the mentoring literature for clues. The good news is—you need not be an "expert" in the conventional sense of the word in order to mentor. All you need is what Bozeman and Feeney (2007) call "unequal knowledge." Allow us to explain with the aid of Exhibit 2-1.

The graphic representation in Exhibit 2-1 displays something usually referred to as a "continuum." At the right end of the continuum is the "expert," and the continuum uses the word in the conventional sense. That is, an "expert" is a person who is widely recognized as knowledgeable about or skillful *in a particular area*. Let's suppose that the area in question is public speaking. An expert in public speaking can, of course, mentor anyone who is a nonexpert (i.e., advanced, intermediate, or beginner). A person at the advanced or intermediate level can mentor also. For example, the person with advanced public speaking skills can mentor the intermediates or the beginners, while the person with intermediate public speaking skills can mentor the beginners. All this is possible because of "unequal knowledge." Refer again to Exhibit 2-1. If your skill or knowledge level is *to the right* of another person's level, you can mentor him or her. Only a beginner cannot mentor anyone. It is, however, unlikely that you are a beginner at everything. We are quite certain that most people have at least some intermediate knowledge or skills in some area. Furthermore, beginners are almost always around, which means plenty of opportunities for mentoring through teaching.

Exhibit 2-1: The Continuum of Expertise in Knowledge or Skills

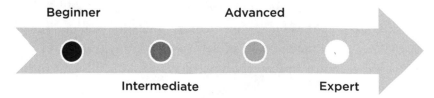

The Job Description: Part 2

Mentees are the prime beneficiaries of mentoring. As such, they're able to tell the difference between great mentoring and so-so mentoring. That's why they are also in a good position to evaluate the correctness of our definition. Asking mentees to critique our output was therefore a no-brainer.

When we did that, a sizeable majority told us that it was incomplete. Specifically, our definition seemed to have left out the *psychological* aspect of mentoring. When pressed for more details, mentees responded with such words as *inspiring* and *encouraging*. Come to think of it, the mentees had a valid point. Many of us have had great teachers, and few of us would have expressed any reservation about using identical or similar words to describe them. Because teaching is a part of mentoring, it makes sense that the great mentors would behave, in some respects, the same way our great teachers did. The behavioral similarities between great mentors and great teachers would, of course, inspire the same kind of admiration and the same kind of characterization.

So, how important is psychological mentoring? Some mentees readily conceded that it did not happen as often as advising or teaching, but it was important nevertheless. One of them provided this insightful comment: "Psychological mentoring is like CPR [cardiopulmonary resuscitation]. Doctors and nurses don't do it every day, but that doesn't mean it isn't important. When the need to deliver the kiss of life arises, the doctor or the nurse physically closest to the patient had better know how to do it!" In other words, psychological mentoring seems to happen as and when it is needed, and its sporadic occurrence should not mislead us into thinking that it is not meaningful. Others, however, pointed out that psychological mentoring can also be described as "ongoing." For example, if one has the good fortune of working closely with a mentor and that mentor is widely admired for her character, one would have plenty of opportunities, perhaps every day, to observe the said character "in action" and be inspired by it. So psychological mentoring can be an ongoing thing. Furthermore, it can be done passively, as the previous example demonstrated: the mentor didn't really do anything; all she did was to be herself. At the same time, it can be done actively, as when a mentor relates his personal success stories to motivate his mentee. In conclusion, psychological mentoring can be sporadic or ongoing, passive or active. Regardless of how it is carried out, psychological mentoring seems to be meaningful to most mentees.

Now that we have more or less ascertained the importance of psychological mentoring, what specific behaviors should be captured in our definition? Here, we found the fire-related idioms and metaphors used by some of the mentees most useful and illustrative. First, when we figuratively "light a fire under" a person, it means that we are able to somehow make that person take action with passion. We call the lighting, that first spark that gets the fire going, *inspiration*. Second, a fire cannot continue burning on its own. If left untended, it will die as a matter of course. So something must be done to keep it burning. When dealing with a real fire, we can fan the flame or add fuel to the fire. But in the world of mentoring, the mentor *motivates* the mentee in order to keep him or her moving toward a growth target. Finally, even if something is being done to keep the fire going, the elements can threaten to extinguish it. The weather is something that people can't control. Sometimes it kills the fire completely, but sometimes it just leaves it nearly dead. If the fire is dead, we can always restart it; and if it's almost dead, we can always do something to bring it back to life. In the same way, the storms of life or work can bring the mentee's growth to a screeching halt or cause it to go off course. Most of the time, these storms do not result in "fatalities." So during such times, the mentor's job is to *encourage* the mentee to continue to press on toward his or her goal despite the challenges. To sum up, *inspiration* serves to get the mentee going, *motivation* serves to keep the mentee going, and *encouragement* serves to keep the mentee going in spite of setbacks (which are bound to occur).

In light of these findings and observations, we decided to expand our initial definition as follows:

A mentor is an advisor and teacher, inspirer,
motivator, and encourager.

We went back to the mentees for another round of verification. This time around, our definition passed muster.

The Job Description: The Finale

Admittedly, our augmented definition is quite a mouthful, so we decided to simplify it. Simplification means that it'll be easier for you to remember. But it's got to be done in a way that doesn't dilute the meaning.

To begin, we can think of both advising and teaching as being closely linked to the achievement of the mentee's goals. More specifically, both advising and teaching *enable* the mentee to achieve his or her goals. Put in a different way, the mentor assumes the role of an *enabler* when he or she advises or teaches.

Inspiration, motivation, and encouragement, on the other hand, keep the mentee from becoming down-and-out. Indeed, mentors are all about helping the mentee to stay up-and-running. We thought the neologism *uplifter* fits the mentor well when he or she is exhibiting any of these behaviors.

So here's our abbreviated and final definition:

A mentor is an enabler and uplifter.

Note that our definition is a *basic* definition of the word *mentor*. The term *basic* suggests that it is both possible and probable for *all* mentors to demonstrate the behaviors described in our definition. Otherwise, they wouldn't be basic. Some, however, may object that several of the behaviors captured in our definition don't seem basic at all. Here's one possible scenario: When people read that to mentor they have to inspire others, some may immediately bow their heads in dejection. Why? Because they think they can *never* do it. Look, inspiring people isn't impossible. Let's consider the facts. First, you're not required to inspire the whole world. You just have to inspire *one* person, your mentee. Second, you don't have to inspire your mentee in any particular way. You can inspire him or her in your own way. One common misconception is that we all need charisma in order to inspire. That's not always true. Consider Bill Gates, the founder of Microsoft. By most accounts, Gates isn't a charismatic person. But talk to software engineers and you are sure to find at least a few who feel inspired by him. If someone can inspire people in his own quiet way, so can you. Finally, some proper training may be in order before the behaviors can happen. But the point is, they *can* happen.

In addition, "basic" means that the behaviors in question can be demonstrated virtually *anywhere*. As far as we know, no insurmountable organizational or cultural barriers prevent those behaviors. Remember that there is no one right way to advise, teach, inspire, motivate, or encourage. As the old saw states, there is more than one way to skin a cat. The methods may be different, but what is most important is that the desired outcome is achieved.

Most of all, do not let our definition limit your thinking and actions in any way. Consider the following example: A mentee approaches a mentor with a question about Vietnam. The mentor responds, "You should talk to Frank Sakamoto about Vietnam. He's the expert. He's also a good friend of mine." By responding thusly, the mentor has actually discharged his duty as advisor to his mentee. He could've just stopped there, and no one can really find fault with that. Or he could personally introduced Frank to his mentee. It's an extra step for the mentor, no doubt, but one that can mean a lot to the mentee. Sometimes, these small things separate great mentors from mediocre ones.

We have so far discussed the *basic* job description of a mentor. Excellence in mentoring, however, usually involves much more than that. It requires, for instance, the ability to help the mentee set his or her long-term goals. Fortunately, these "extras" can be learned. In the subsequent chapters, you will learn knowledge, skills, and techniques that will enhance your overall mentoring ability.

Going the Extra Mile

When *some* mentors learned of our final definition, they responded that they did more than what our definition said, especially in terms of enablement.

"What were those extras?" was, of course, our question. Two behaviors were highlighted:

- Sponsorship: The opening of doors that would otherwise be closed to the mentee; it includes making special opportunities available to them.
- Protection: The shielding of the mentee from the damage that organizational members can potentially inflict on them.

What is our response to these "extras"? If you recall, our "basic" definition implies that every mentor can demonstrate the mentoring behaviors stated in the definition, and that those behaviors can be demonstrated practically anywhere. We readily acknowledge that behaviors such as sponsorship and protection are mentioned in the classical mentoring literature (e.g., the works of Dr. Kathy Kram). Recent research, however, suggests that it is not possible for *all* mentors to demonstrate sponsorship or protection behaviors.

Let us first consider sponsorship. Sponsorship is difficult these days because of the short supply of special opportunities in many of today's organizations, as Harvard Business School professor Thomas DeLong and his colleagues point out (DeLong, Gabarro, and Lees, 2008). Hence, not every mentor is able to make such opportunities available to a mentee. That means sponsorship isn't basic enough to be included in our definition.

What about protection? Research shows that the benefits of protection are, at best, uncertain. Indeed, Australian researchers Fowler and O'Gorman (2005) have drawn attention to the negative correlations between protection and several growth indicators (e.g., salary, promotion). Furthermore, using empirical data, they've shown that protection appears to be *absent* at today's workplaces in Australia.

Although Australia isn't the whole world, their research suggests that protection may not be a common behavior these days. In view of this finding, we find little reason to incorporate protection into our definition.

The question, then, is this: "You are a mentor, and you have been exhibiting the behaviors in question for quite some time. Should you continue doing so?" To be honest, we see nothing inherently wrong with what you're doing. So, if you can do it and you really want to, then we think it's OK for you to continue. But if you have more than one mentee at the same time, some circumspection is in order. If your behaviors are perceived to benefit one mentee much more than the other, you could end up in trouble. Allegations of favoritism are likely to be hurled at you. Moreover, your behaviors, no matter how well-intentioned, could inadvertently harm your mentees. Therefore, exercise caution.

Another danger is that your mentee *expects* you to sponsor, protect, or do both. Like you, your mentee has access to the mentoring literature and they could have been exposed to the two ideas and they may desire them. An insidious side to this issue happens when your mentee harbors such a desire and you are completely unaware of it. As you will probably agree, unfulfilled expectations are a ticking time bomb. The way to defuse it is to get everyone's expectations on the table—the earlier in the mentoring relationship, the better—and to deal with them head-on. We will address this issue in a later chapter.

Activity: Taking Inventory

Ask yourself this question: What can I offer to a mentee? Your answer will help determine your ability to mentor.

To help you with the question, we have developed a two-page Mentor Profile Form (see Exhibit 2-2). Respond up to the "Hobbies and Interests" Section for this activity. You may finish the rest after reading Chapter 3.

Exhibit 2-2: Mentor Profile Form

KSAs

Name:	Date:
Current position:	
Current responsibilities:	
How long have you worked in this position?	
How long have you worked in this company?	
Previous employer(s), if any (please state):	
List key knowledge, skills, and abilities (KSAs) required to perform your job. Include both technical and "soft" KSAs.	
What knowledge, skills, and abilities do you believe you excel at? (Use list from above.)	

(continued)

Academic Information

Post-secondary academic information		
Diploma/Degree	School	Graduation Year

Training Information

Training (in-house and external) information

Please provide a summary of the training in which you have participated that you believe to be highly relevant to your current job.

Hobbies and Interests (please state)

Mentor's expectations and concerns

What do you hope to gain by becoming a mentor?

What do you look for in a mentee? What knowledge, skills, abilities, or personality traits must he or she have?

In what ways can you help your mentee the most?

What do you foresee as the major obstacles you will encounter in providing quality mentoring?

CHAPTER 3

THE WILLINGNESS FACTOR

"Where the willingness is great, the difficulties cannot be great."
—Niccolo Machiavelli, Italian writer and philosopher

The Missing Ingredient

When you're mentoring someone, you are either involved in a mentoring interaction or a mentoring relationship.

In a mentoring interaction, you just happened (or were asked) to be at the right place, at the right time, and had the ability to offer valuable help to somebody. Typically, no-strings-attached applies in this sort of thing. You don't commit to anything, you don't expect anything back, and you may never even meet the mentee again. You just wanted to help, and in that one particular instance, you could, and you did. Practically anyone can "do" a mentoring interaction. You don't need to read a book or get trained for it.

A mentoring relationship, on the other hand, is much more complex. It consists of a series of mentoring interactions with the same mentee. These interactions are connected to the mentee's goal or goals, and they are frequent and intense. The duration of the relationship isn't always fixed; it could last for months or sometimes years. It will entail investments on the part of the mentor, sometimes substantial ones, in terms of time, energy, and resources. It is essentially a medium- to long-term commitment to the mentee's growth.

Many of today's organizations are interested in mentors who are capable of doing *both* kinds of mentoring. The question is: Are you ready for the relationship kind?

It can be a difficult question to answer. To better understand it, let's do a short thought experiment. Let's suppose that you were asked to consider mentoring someone called Jill. Jill is new to the company. And Jill is a total stranger to you. You were given some information about her, but not much. Let's also suppose that you're a veteran mentor with plenty of experience, and that you're absolutely sure you have transmittable content Jill would find useful. Finally, let's suppose that you had a choice in the matter—you could say yes or no without the possibility of any punitive action against you, either now or in the future. Given those circumstances, what would your answer be? Our guess is, some of you will say yes and some of you will say no. Why doesn't everyone say yes (or no, for that matter)? In our little experiment, we've thrown into the decision-making mix *ability* and *experience,* but the two are not enough. Let's face it: Just because you can do something doesn't automatically mean that you want to. Something is missing, and we call it the *willingness factor*. This chapter is all about this ingredient.

The Willingness Factor

The willingness factor is, arguably, the most important ingredient in the decision-making mix. Among the three—ability, experience, and willingness—it is the one that will most likely get you to say yes to a mentoring relationship.

Generally, mentors say yes when they are reasonably confident the relationship will succeed. How they reach those decisions is highly personal. You likely have your own way of deliberating as well. In short, the willingness factor is all about you. It is your reason or reasons for wanting to get involved in a mentoring relationship.

So, what's your willingness factor?

To help you with the question, we have developed a tool called "Discovering Your Reasons to Mentor" (see Exhibit 3-1).

Exhibit 3-1: Discovering Your Reasons to Mentor

Instructions

1. Think about why you want to become a mentor and review the following statements. If you agree with a statement, place a check mark next to it, under the Agree column. If you disagree with a statement, simply leave the space next to it blank. *There are no wrong answers.*

2. Review all the statements you checked, and select the *top three.* Then give each of those three reasons one of the following point values: 90, 60, and 30. Use the scale shown here when assigning points. *Please do so honestly and thoughtfully.*

   90 points: The most important reason
   60 points: The second most important reason
   30 points: The third most important reason

	Statement	Agree	Points
1	"I am entering into a mentoring relationship because I am interested in mentoring a particular person."		
2	"Mentoring offers me an opportunity for collaborative learning."		
3	"Mentoring gives me an opportunity to work with people who are different from me."		
4	"I see mentoring as an opportunity to further my own growth and development."		
5	"I see mentoring as an opportunity to enhance my visibility and reputation in my organization."		
6	"I see mentoring as an opportunity to advance my own career."		
7	"I see mentoring as a way to help build the organization."		
8	"I am entering into a mentoring relationship because I am committed to my organization's succession planning."		

(continued)

	Statement	Agree	Points
9	"I am entering into a mentoring relationship because it's part of my job description."		
10	"I am entering into a mentoring relationship because I need to meet a performance requirement."		
11	Other (Add your own reason or reasons if you cannot find yours on this list. Do not exceed the maximum number of three "agrees.")		

The tool contains a list of possible—and real—reasons for mentoring. The list, to be sure, isn't comprehensive. As much as we would like to, we are unable to provide you with an exhaustive one because the diversity of reasons is enormous. As the sixteenth-century French writer Montaigne once observed, "There never were in the world two opinions alike, no more than two hairs or two grains; the most universal quality is diversity." The list, however, does include many of the common reasons why mentors enter into mentoring relationships. We are therefore confident that you will find yours among them. If you still can't, feel free to add your own reason(s). (See the bottom row of the tool for more information.)

You should realize that your reasons aren't immutable. That is, they may vary from situation to situation. For example, in situation A, your reasons for mentoring were W and X, but in situation B, your reasons may be Y and Z. It is therefore recommended that you use the tool whenever you are contemplating initiating a mentoring relationship with a new mentee.

Let us pause here and let you discover your reason(s) before we move any further. Take your time and don't rush through it. There are no wrong answers. All that is required are honest and thoughtful responses.

Note: You may also wish to complete the remainder of the Mentor Profile Form (see Exhibit 2-2 in the previous chapter) at this juncture.

Give Your Willingness a Boost

The tool shown in Exhibit 3-1 helps you to determine your reasons to mentor through a round of self-reflection. You now know the main reasons behind your desire to mentor and how much each of them means to you (refer to your point values).

But our tool is ultimately about much more. It can, in fact, help you to decide whether a mentee is "right" for you.

Here are a few ways in which it can assist you in that regard:

- If the statement "Mentoring offers me an opportunity for collaborative learning" or the statement "I see mentoring as an opportunity to further my own growth and development" is your most important reason to mentor, you will want a mentee who can give as well as they take. If the learning is all one-way (that is, the learning always passes from you to the mentee and rarely the other way round), you will be an unhappy and unwilling mentor.

- If the statement "I see mentoring as an opportunity to enhance my visibility and reputation in my organization" is your top priority, you will want a mentee with high ability or potential. If his or her ability or potential increases the chances of his or her becoming a superstar, you will likely gain the visibility and reputation that you're looking for when your mentee does become one. Hence, if this description fits you, you probably won't be a happy and willing mentor if your mentee does not have at least some star qualities.

- If the statement "Mentoring gives me an opportunity to work with people who are different from me" is your main motivation, you will then want a mentee who has a personality, ethnicity, or style different from yours. Otherwise, you may end up being an unhappy and reluctant mentor.

We can give you more examples, but we think you get the picture. Indeed, having the right mentee will significantly boost your overall willingness to mentor. And that is what our tool is ultimately about—to help you get the right mentee.

However, getting the right mentee isn't a straightforward process. As you can see in the preceding examples, a degree of *specificity* is involved. And the degree varies from mentor to mentor. It can be highly specific, as the statement "I am entering into a mentoring relationship because I am interested in mentoring a *particular* person" suggests. Or it can be a specific *type* of mentee, as the three earlier illustrations indicate. Or it can be *general*, as the statement "I see mentoring as a way to help build the organization" implies. Remember the thought experiment involving the imaginary newcomer, Jill? We predicted that some people would say yes. Some mentors aren't especially selective; they just want to help somebody, period. Those who said no in our thought experiment were clearly more selective, but we cannot fault them for behaving that way. Bear in mind that every mentorship is fundamentally a relationship. Like all serious and deep relationships, it factors in compatibility. For some people, such compatibility decisions can't be rushed: They need time to think through them. We can all perhaps learn something about compatibility from another kind of human relationship—romantic relationships. Consider this question: Why do two people date or court before they walk down the aisle and say "I do" to each other? One reasonable answer is that they use premarital relationships to help them determine whether their partner is compatible with themselves. Because compatibility plays a part in successful marriages, romantic partners don't seem to mind investing some time and resources in exploring this issue. If a girl can't just marry any Tom, Dick, or Harry, and a man just doesn't marry any Mary, Jane, or Susie, some mentors in the same way just can't mentor anybody or everybody. They first want to be sure that their mentee is compatible with themselves; some may even consider the question of compatibility over the long haul (in view of the possibility that mentoring can be a long-term relationship). So such mentors need time and want time to contemplate these weighty issues. Therefore, it comes as no surprise that some people don't rush into mentoring relationships. To them, entering into a mentoring relationship with the wrong person is like marrying the wrong person.

If you use our tool (Exhibit 3-1) correctly, you will recognize what compatibility issues are important to you, and you will want to explore them with your prospective mentee. A good way to do so is to establish a platonic, nonmentoring relationship with your prospect, sort of like a date without the romance, before the two of you enter into the real thing. You can, for instance, ask the prospect out for a meal or two and get to know him or her better. If you are fearful of gossip, you can invite your prospect along in a group setting, which is less likely to set tongues wagging.

When It's OK to Say No

Clearly, one of the most important decisions you'll ever make as a mentor is whether to enter into a mentoring relationship with a particular person. The wrong decision can harm the mentee as well as yourself—you will be an unhappy and unwilling mentor with, at best, a lukewarm interest to help the mentee to grow. It also suggests that it is OK for a mentor to say no at times to a relationship, especially when you have a legitimate reason for doing so (and not an *excuse* to wriggle out of mentoring).

So, when is it OK to say no?

Not surprisingly, incompatibility is a good reason to say no. It comes in several forms. Here are some of them:

Mentee Unreadiness

Consider the following story:

As a university professor and noted author, I am often approached via e-mail by people who've read my books. These people are from many other countries. They usually ask if I would be their mentor. I always answer, and I always say I would be willing to be their mentor. Then I ask, "How can I help?" Few of them send me a subsequent e-mail to answer that question!

Those people who never got back to the professor were basically unready. They didn't lack confidence, to be sure. After all, they were the ones who approached the professor, not the other way round. However, their actions suggest they may have made an assumption—a wrong one—that the professor, the candidate mentor, is the person responsible for driving the mentorship forward.

This example is not how mentoring works, especially in the early part of the relationship. At that critical juncture, the mentee is the one in the driver's seat, not the mentor. All prospective mentees must know what they want and how they want to be helped so that others will know how to help them. In practical terms, it usually means that the prospective mentee has to come up with at least a tentative goal, a provisional plan for achieving that goal, and a rough idea about how the candidate mentor can fit into the scheme of things. The goal, plan, and fit need not be perfect—all the candidate mentor *should* want to see is that the prospective mentee has thought things through. We'll discuss this beginning goal formulation in detail in one of the following chapters.

Mentoring at Yum! Brands

At Yum! Brands, the assumption is that each employee must take responsibility for his or her own development. Mentoring is a means to that end. Mentoring is encouraged during the onboarding process. Mentoring supports transmission of corporate culture and values and factors in the strategic planning process. But perhaps the most visible use of mentoring is to support implementation of Individual Development Plans (IDPs) as part of the succession planning and talent management effort. Intended to build individual engagement and thereby reduce turnover of highly talented people, mentoring is not limited to face-to-face efforts and does occur across international boundaries. Mentoring is low cost but potentially high impact in its emphasis on interpersonal relationships.

Source: Adapted from R. Emelo, "Conversations with mentoring leaders." *T + D* (June 2011): 35.

The bottom line: If you're approached by a prospect who hasn't done any groundwork, or not enough of it, just say no.

Cross-Purposes

If your prospect is unable or unwilling to help you to fulfill the reasons behind your desire to mentor, especially the ones important to you, the two of you are in a real sense at cross-purposes. In this situation, you should not to enter into a mentoring relationship.

Some of your reasons are "missions possible" (e.g., collaborative learning), but some may be more difficult to fulfill. Take the case of enhanced visibility and reputation. No prospect or mentee can ever *guarantee* they'll be able to enhance, either directly or indirectly, the mentor's visibility and reputation. In such cases, the mentor may have to adjust his or her own expectations somewhat.

Ability Mismatch

When what you can offer is not what the prospect or mentee needs or wants, you have a case of *ability mismatch*, and you should say no. (The contents of your Mentor Profile Form should give you a good idea of what you can currently offer.) Ability mismatch can occur even when the mentor has content that seems "relevant" to the mentee's needs but the knowledge between the two of them is far too *unequal* (see Chapter 2). Imagine what will happen when a mentor at the expert level and a mentee at the beginner level are paired up. Such a mentoring relationship isn't likely to work out. When that gap seems excessively wide, say no in a nice way.

Values Clash

Values are what you consider to be important in life. (Life, of course, encompasses work.) If you and your prospect (or mentee) can't see eye to eye on values, you should part ways amicably and say no to each other.

Here is an extreme scenario to drive home this point. Based on some fascinating work done by Carlo Morselli at the University of Montreal in Canada and his colleagues, we've learned that criminals have mentors too. Their data show that mentored criminals make more money than nonmentored ones.

You will obviously need to discover your prospect's or mentee's values. But you should know your values first. Here is an activity to help you discover yours, and you begin by answering at least two of the following questions (the more, the better):

1. *Whom do you admire? (Your hero or heroine can be a fictional character or a real human being. If he or she is real, they can either be living or deceased.)*
2. *Whose company do you enjoy the most?*
3. *How do you spend your money?*
4. *How do you use your leisure time?*

When you have answered the questions, ask yourself a few follow-up questions to identify your values. One great follow-up question is "Why do I do this?" For example, "Why do I admire so-and-so?" or "Why I do spend my money this way?"

I admire so-and-so because _____.

You may need to ask the "Why do I do this?" question several times to get to the bottom of things (i.e., to identify your value). That is, you may have to further question your "because" responses. You should, however, restrict yourself to a maximum of five "Why" questions.

Finally, look for similar values across your answers to the different questions. If you discover a pattern, those similarities indicate your **core values**—*"principles without which [your] life wouldn't be worth living," as someone has put it.*

We mentioned earlier that you must discover your prospect's (or mentee's) values. The earlier you do so, the better for the two of you, because you can then decide whether to move forward or part ways. But let's not kid ourselves—discovering a prospect's values can sometimes be a challenge. People tend to play their cards close to their chests, especially in the early stages of a relationship. Because of this tendency, you will of course have to be subtle in your approach. A good time to talk about values is to do it during the so-called dating period. And a good way to get the right sort of conversation going is for the mentor is to self-disclose. To self-disclose is to reveal personal information that is usually kept secret. When one party self-discloses, the other party will most likely reciprocate by self-disclosing. Begin your self-disclosure by telling the prospect a personal story, for instance, one about a significant experience and explain why it is significant to you. Then prompt the prospect to reciprocate. Say something like, "How about you? What significant experiences have affected you?" Finally, if the values remain unclear, sneak in some questions that are similar to the Why questions mentioned earlier. You could also discover your prospect's values through your knowledge of their goals. You, of course, have to get them talking about their goals first, which is often not difficult. Then say something like, "That's an interesting goal. May I know why you're pursuing it?" These steps and approach will help you discover your prospect's values.

No Time

Mentors can be busy people. Their workload can be heavy. They may need to travel a lot. They may have family commitments as well. If you can't find the time to do a mentoring job well, just say no. It is absolutely acceptable to be realistic about time commitments. But no one is busy all the time. So when you have enough downtime, do say yes.

How to Say No the Right Way

Given the constraints that they constantly face, mentors must entertain the real possibility of saying no. Some mentors find it difficult to do. Who can blame them? It's almost like rejecting a date! Here's the good news—it's possible to say no in a nice way. It's not only a nice thing to do, it's also the right thing.

Here's a true story about a prospecting mentee who got rejected and still felt good about her rejection:

It was one of the biggest trade shows for our industry, and the who's who were all there. One of my heroines was there too. I thought to myself it would be a great opportunity to network with her, maybe even persuade her to mentor me. It was a gutsy move. I mean, I didn't know anything about this person, I just knew about her achievements, which were outstanding. Nevertheless, I told myself, nothing ventured, nothing gained. So I plucked up the courage to talk with her. And you know what, she was really nice about the whole thing. She told me it wasn't a good time to talk then. She said, how about later that evening, talk over a cup of coffee? I of course said yes.

When evening came, she was there at the coffee shop, waiting for me. I mean, I wasn't late, she was early. Anyway, we had a good time talking. She listened. She asked questions. And when I raised the question about mentoring, she said she wouldn't make a good mentor for anyone at that particular point in time because she was traveling a lot. When I heard that, I felt a little disappointed. But, somehow, the way she said it made it possible for me to recover quickly. She then said she knew someone who may be able to help me with my specific needs, but she said she couldn't promise me much. She could only promise to connect me with this other person. And that she did. That person eventually became my mentor for about three years. Anyway, when we finished our coffee, I realized that we had been talking for almost an hour! Time just flew by because we were enjoying ourselves.

We asked the prospecting mentee: "Why did you feel good about that experience?"

"She rejected me respectfully," she replied.

When we revisit her story, we find that the candidate mentor did indeed show the prospecting mentee respect. Here are some of the behavioral indicators:

1. The candidate mentor was polite to the mentee.
2. She was punctual for her meeting.
3. She listened.

As you can see, all those behaviors are the so-called little things in life. "[In] relationships, the little things are the big things," writes renowned management author, Stephen R. Covey.

So when you have to say no, pay attention to the "little things." Be nice, and don't be a jerk.

And if you can't mentor a person, do the next best thing—connect the prospect with someone in your network you think is ready to mentor.

The Road Ahead

The willingness factor is about whether to initiate a mentoring relationship. If you say yes, it simply means your journey as a mentor has only just begun. You will still have plenty of work to do to help the mentee grow. In the second part of our book, we talk about this important subject in more detail.

PART II

THE HOW-TO OF MENTORING

CHAPTER 4

MENTORING: THE STORY

"Though analogy is often misleading, it is the least misleading thing we have."
—Samuel Butler, eighteenth-century English writer

The Story Analogy

In the first part of the book, you learned about the fundamentals of mentoring, which means you already know what you're supposed to do.

The next part is all about how to do what you're supposed to do. But before we get into the how-to, it's good for you to have a sense of how the relationship *should* unfold. We devote this chapter to doing just that.

Note that we used the word *should* and not *must*. It's a suggestion, not a commandment. The mentor *must*, however, maintain appropriate flexibility in any and every mentoring relationship, because every relationship is dynamic and unique. Put in another way, no two relationships are exactly alike. They differ in two major ways. First, they differ from mentor to mentor. For example, the way A mentors B is different from the way Y mentors Z. Second, they differ because there is no one right way to mentor—the same mentor can choose to mentor two different mentees in two different ways. For example, the way A mentors B is different from the way A mentors C.

Flexibility, however, doesn't mean good mentoring occurs in a chaotic, haphazard way. In fact, what we are about to propose here is a fairly well-defined framework. At the same time that room for flexibility is important, what happens within a mentorship should make coherent sense and contribute to the mentee's growth or, at the very least, not harm it.

In light of this need for both flexibility and structure, we encourage you to think analogically. An *analogy* is "a comparison between one thing and another, typically for the purpose of explanation or clarification." Indeed, a good analogy can help you see or think about things more clearly. An analogy offers you guidance and direction and, at the same time, flexibility. In short, it can give you the best of both worlds, just right for a complicated phenomenon like mentoring.

The question is: What makes a good analogy for mentoring? After much thought, we settled on story making. Why? First, we see similarities between mentoring and stories; we'll reveal these similarities as we go along. Second, many of us enjoy a great story—it is something we ourselves have experienced and can readily relate to. Together, these factors make stories a productive way to think about mentoring.

Hence, for the rest of this chapter, we will look at mentoring as story making. The analogy provides the mentor with a big-picture view of the mentorship. At the same time, it offers some related themes that will shed light on the intricacies of mentoring.

The Mentoring "Story"

A conventional story has a beginning, a middle, and an end. We think it's also useful for mentors to think of mentoring as having these three phases. Also, a good beginning increases the chances of a good middle, and a good beginning and middle increase the chances of a good end.

We call the beginning the Establishing phase. In this phase, both the mentor and mentee work together to lay the foundation for a productive and potentially long-term relationship. The key activity of this phase is what we call "goal-refining." It will be covered in the detail in the next chapter.

The middle is called the Enabling-and-Uplifting phase. During this time the enablement and uplifting that we talked about in Chapter 3 occur. In several of the later chapters, you will learn powerful mentoring techniques—reflection, modeling, and storytelling—that will elevate your overall mentoring effectiveness.

Finally, the end phase is called the Exiting phase. It happens when the mentor and the mentee go their separate ways. The mentor exits when he or she can no longer contribute meaningfully to the mentee's growth. We can also look at the same situation from another perspective: The mentee has reached the point where he or she can longer benefit from the mentor's enablement. Most important of all, when both partners agree that they have indeed reached this point, they should separate and exit the relationship. The exit should not occur haphazardly. It should be properly planned out. It is unfortunate that many mentors do not do so, resulting in either a turbulent end or a prolonged dependency. A later chapter is dedicated to the subject of exiting. There, we show you how to exit in ways that are good for both you and your mentee.

The three phases are displayed in Exhibit 4-1.

Within this fairly well-defined three-phase framework, the mentor should put on his or her story-maker cap and exercise an appropriate

Exhibit 4-1: The Three Phases of Mentoring

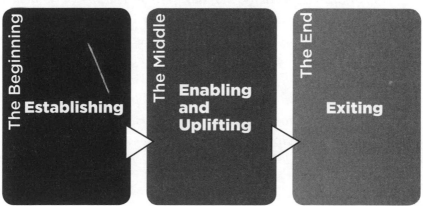

amount of "artistic license," which is the flexibility we referred to earlier. Hence, do not be afraid to make adjustments, if and when appropriate. For example, if you see the need to uplift your mentee in the Establishing phase, just do it. If, for appropriate reasons, you have to exit after only several sessions, you do that too.

All mentors must recognize that mentoring, like real life, doesn't follow a script. That is, you can never be fully prepared for *everything* in mentoring. You are likely to find surprises down the road. Mentoring will throw you a curveball every now and then. When it happens, you'll have to ad lib or improvise to deal with it.

This point about the inherent unpredictability of mentoring and life reminds us of a story that Sir Michael Parkinson, the famous BBC (British Broadcasting Corporation) television show host, recently shared with his audience. Sir Michael did not start out famous. Like most people, he had to work hard to succeed. In the early days of his career, he had to work especially hard. One of his strategies was to get big-name celebrities to come on his show, but it was difficult then because he lacked the star power to pull them in. Nevertheless, he managed to persuade the legendary U.S. filmmaker, Orson Welles, to be one of his first guests.

Just before their interview, the two men had an extraordinary conversation:

Orson Welles enters young Michael Parkinson's room and introduces himself. Parkinson, somewhat nervous, responds accordingly. Welles sees several sheets of paper on the desk. "That?" he asks. "My questions," the host replies succinctly. The filmmaker asks politely whether he can have a look at them. The host duly obliges. He picks them up and looks at them for a few moments. He then asks Parkinson for the number of shows he already has under his belt. "Two," the answer comes back. Welles informs Parkinson that he has done "many more." "Will you take my advice?" the filmmaker offers. The host agrees. All of a sudden, Welles tears up everything and says to Parkinson point-blank, "Let's talk."

Sir Michael later revealed that he adopted Welles's advice and gave credit to the filmmaker for his show's success.

Mentors would also do well to heed Welles's advice. If you adhere slavishly to your plan, you may miss the wonderful opportunities that emerge along the way. Therefore, don't overprepare—play things by ear.

In contrast, some aspiring or inexperienced mentors have approached us for what can be called "a mentoring screenplay." (In movie talk, the screenplay is the script plus the acting instructions; actors and actresses read the screenplay, memorize their lines, and play their parts.) These mentors want such a thing because they want to "get it right." The reason behind the request is noble. But our advice to them is this: Don't get one. We say this for three reasons. The first is the same as the Orson Welles's advice: Play things by ear. The second: Such a screenplay is either nonexistent or bare-bones minimal in mentoring. Script fragments, if you will, are scattered throughout the mentoring literature, but it is unlikely that a complete script can be found. The third: Even if you can find a complete script, it may not be the right one for your situation. For example, a culturally "Western" script may not work in the East.

So, let go, to a degree, and have an authentic, down-to-earth conversation with your mentee. Having said that, we are not so mean as to leave you in the deep end. (Hey! We're mentors too and we're here to help.) So throughout the second part of the book, we sprinkle some must-ask questions and must-do things. How you fill in the remaining blanks is up to you.

Coauthors

You should note that in every mentoring "story," there are two story makers—you and your mentee. As implied in the previous chapter, your mentee should be the lead author. After all, it is largely his or her "story," not yours. But that doesn't mean the mentor never leads. Indeed, at times, you must lead. You lead because you have knowledge, skills, and insights that the mentee doesn't. You lead not because you want to, but because you have to. In short, the two partners have to be flexible about who leads and when.

Can a situation with two heads lead to chaos? Yes, it can. A Turkish saying describes the possible consequences: "Two captains sink the ship." To avoid misunderstandings or conflicts, roles and responsibilities must be clearly determined during the Establishing phase. Negotiations between the two partners over a variety of issues are important, and they should be preceded by a healthy amount of constructive talking and listening.

The Influencers

When we make stories, we rarely, if ever, begin with a blank slate. For example, we draw inspiration from our own experiences or the experiences of others. Or perhaps we are so inspired by our favorite authors that we want to imitate the way they make stories. In other words, story makers may not be entirely free from outside or inside influences.

The same is true of mentoring. Forces both inside and out can influence the way we mentor. Hence, while mentors strive for flexibility, they may not be completely flexible at times. If the influences are positive and beneficial, then it's OK. But, sometimes, these influences can be negative and harmful. So we have to remain vigilant. The thing is, these factors can work at either the conscious or subconscious level. If it's subconscious, it means that you may not even be aware that they are at work. How do we resist them, then? The first step is to become aware of them. A good way to gain such awareness is to learn about them.

At least three (and we are sure there are more) such factors merit our consideration here. They are as follows:

- Education
- Experience
- Edict

Education

By education, we mean your prior training and/or personal reading. If you have attended a training program in mentoring, what you've learned from it will probably influence the way you mentor. In addition, like many of today's mentors, you have access to the growing body of mentoring literature, and in all likelihood, you've been exposed to it. All that you have absorbed from your reading is likely to influence how you mentor too.

Education is good, but one must always question the practical implications of what one has learned. Consider this possibility: What you have learned may have worked somewhere else, but it may not necessarily work in the here and now. For example, you read about the benefits of mentoring in a book and you want to implement it organization-wide, but in reality, your workplace as a whole may not be ready for it. If your organization, for instance, doesn't truly value learning, then organization-wide mentoring will most likely fail.

Experience

The second factor is experience. If you are an experienced mentor, your prior experiences as one will influence your approach to mentoring. Your prior experiences as a mentee will do the same thing also.

Here is how experience may direct you: What you view as positive experiences, you will probably want to recreate in your mentorships; and what you view as negative, you will want to avoid. For instance, if you find stories beneficial, you will probably want to tell more stories. If you find your former mentor's downloading annoying, you may want to inject more coaching into your mentoring.

Experience can be helpful, but it can also work against you. For instance, something worked for you in the past, but that same thing may not necessarily work in the here and now. Consider this: You greatly enjoyed a prior mentorship that included plenty of downloading, but today you are in a relationship with a high achiever. You have to entertain the possibility that downloading may be inappropriate in your current situation.

Edict

No human relationship takes place in a vacuum. Neither does mentoring. Indeed, all mentoring relationships occur against a context, be it a community or business entity.

Most contexts, if not all, have what we loosely call "edicts." An edict is a rule with a commandment-like quality. Noncompliance may not affect your eternal destiny, but it can certainly get you into earthly trouble.

If we think analogically, company policies are like edicts. They are a company's explicitly stated rules, and you are expected to know them and adhere to them. In addition, nonadherence can mean getting fired. Although your handbook may not contain a section dedicated to mentoring, certain parts of it can still be highly relevant. For example, if you are involved in a cross-gender mentoring relationship, you might want to read up on your company's sexual harassment policies.

Not all edicts are stated, however. The so-called unwritten rules are an integral part of a company's culture. Culture refers to the way things are done or the things that are expected at an organization. If you are an intraorganizational (i.e., in-house) mentor with an intraorganizational mentee, you will probably be influenced by your company's culture. For example, if your company expects its mentors to be content experts, you are more likely to behave as one and perform frequent downloading. On the other hand, if your company expects its mentors to be coachlike, you will probably adopt a less directive approach and ask more probing questions.

Speaking of expectations, you should note that what your company expects of your mentee may not be right for him or her. Let's say you are involved in your company's mentoring program and its objective is talent retention. What if, after much discussion with your mentee and after much reflection on your part, you reach the conclusion that your company isn't the right place for him or her? The right thing is to let your mentee know that the grass is truly greener somewhere else.

Another way companies can exert control over the way you mentor is through something called "formal mentoring." To better understand formal mentoring, we have to first understand its counterpart, informal mentoring. Informal mentoring is purportedly the way mentoring was practiced in the past. In the old days, mentoring meant two people pairing up of their own accord. They both decided on the agenda of their relationship, without outside interference. In other words, everything was rather informal—hence, *informal mentoring*. When mentoring first made it into the modern workplace, it retained many of its informal features. Many high achievers have in recent times claimed that mentoring is instrumental to their success. The title of a *Harvard Business Review* article—"Everyone Who Makes It Has a Mentor"—captures these sentiments quite nicely. Organizations bought into the idea and took it a step farther: They seek to amplify the benefits of informal mentoring organization-wide. As a result, formal mentoring programs are created. Formal mentoring is essentially an organizational intervention. Like most interventions, it has objectives that guide and direct your mentoring. They are generally harmless, as long as they don't work against the growth of your mentee, which is the core purpose of mentoring.

The main point about the influencers is this: You cannot let them control your every move like a puppet master. You should create your mentoring "story" the way you see fit.

The following story describes standing up for one's beliefs while mentoring:

When I was a manager at an insurance company, one of my direct subordinates came to me and said that she wanted my job. I was not offended; on the contrary, I was flattered and said I would do all in my power to help. I informed my own supervisor about what had happened. He was, however, not supportive. He told me the employee was disloyal. I asked how that could be if she had worked for the company for more than 20 years. He answered that she had moved divisions many times, not always with the support of her immediate supervisor, and that was his definition of disloyalty. I could not have disagreed more, and I told him so. I said that it was a good thing to move around to parts of the business to receive exposure and that such movement was the reason for job rotations of managers. I told my worker what my boss had said and that I would help her qualify for my job—perhaps in another company! I strongly value people who want to develop themselves. As director of learning at the company, I also felt that I should set the example that I would like to see other managers follow. So my subordinate and I met periodically to discuss her career goals and development needs. One of the things I did was to update my own job description and then sat down with her to discuss what I believed she could do—and what she could not—and gave her suggestions on how to develop in areas where she could not perform the work I was doing.

The bottom line: You must challenge the influences if and when necessary. First, be aware of them. If they make sense to you after some contemplation, comply. If they don't, have the courage to fight them.

Do some self-reflection by completing the worksheets in Exhibits 4-2 and 4-3.

Exhibit 4-2: A Worksheet to Surface Mentoring Expectations

Directions: Use this worksheet to help you surface your expectations as a mentor. For each question posed in the left column, provide some answers in the right column. Be prepared to share your expectations with those who ask you to be a mentor.

	Questions About Your Expectations as a Prospective Mentor	Your Notes/Answers
1	What do you expect you should do as a mentor?	
2	What do you expect that you should not do as a mentor?	
3	What do you expect of a mentee?	
4	What do you expect that a mentee should not do?	
5	What experience have you had with other people mentoring you? Were those good experiences? If so, what was good about them? Were those bad experiences? If so, what was bad about them?	
6	What factors do you believe are most important in an effective mentoring relationship? Why?	

Exhibit 4.3: A Worksheet to Surface Mentee Expectations

Directions: Use this worksheet to help you surface your expectations as a mentee. For each question posed in the left column, provide some answers in the right column. Be prepared to share your expectations with those whom you seek out as a mentor.

	Questions About Your Expectations as a Prospective Mentee	Your Notes/Answers
1	What do you expect of a mentor?	
2	What do you not expect of a mentor?	
3	What do you believe you should expect to do as a mentee?	
4	What do you expect that you should not do as a mentee?	
5	What experience have you had with other people mentoring you? Were those good experiences? If so, what was good about them? Were those bad experiences? If so, what was bad about them?	
6	What factors do you believe are most important in an effective mentoring relationship? Why?	

Mentoring at McDonald's

McDonald's has long used mentoring. It is not limited to employees but also includes franchise holders and suppliers as well. For four years McDonald's has had a virtual mentoring program that encourages people to interact even when they are not face-to-face. Mentoring proceeds at a pace that is desirable to both mentor and mentee. No set framework or structure binds people to the mentoring relationship; rather, mentoring is one way to encourage continuous learning and continuous company improvement.

Source: Adapted from R. Emelo, "Conversations with mentoring leaders." *T + D* (June 2011): 35.

Concluding Remarks

In this chapter, you've learned about the importance of being appropriately flexible in mentoring. Certain situations or influences can, however, restrict the flexibility we strive for. We should be aware of them, and we should resist them when they are negative and harmful. At the end of the day, all mentors must remain true to the core purpose of mentoring, which is the growth of the mentee.

CHAPTER 5

LAYING THE FOUNDATION

"Good beginnings promise a good end."
—English proverb

Start Strong, Finish Strong

Every sensible person wants to finish strong. In the context of mentoring relationships, it means having a relationship that is highly productive and possibly long term. How can mentors improve their chances of achieving this end result?

Conventional wisdom suggests that if you want to finish strong, you've got to start strong. For example, the ancient Greek philosopher Plato asserts that "[the] beginning is the most important part of the work," and an old English proverb teaches us that "a good beginning makes a good ending." Even moderns such as Stephen Covey recommend something similar—"Begin with the end in mind."

The anecdotal evidence that we've collected suggests the same thing. So, it's safe to say that good beginnings are important for effective mentoring relationships. But don't get us wrong here. We are not saying that a good beginning *guarantees* a good ending. What we're saying is a good ending is *more likely* when the beginning is good. We're certain that every well-meaning mentor would want to increase his or her chances of ending well. That's why we've come up with this chapter about beginnings just for such mentors. Specifically, it's about how to have good beginnings in your mentoring relationships.

The beginning is, of course, connected to the Establishing phase we talked about in the previous chapter. As mentioned, the principal activity in this phase is goal-refining. In this chapter, we'll talk about the goal-refining process. You will also learn here several important relationship-related principles and practices. They are all about how a mentor can establish a mentorship on a firm footing.

An important note before we end the introduction: Not every beginning is the same. For example, you may already know your mentee well, or you could be complete strangers to each other. The first extreme is highly probable in informal mentoring; whereas the other extreme is likely in formal mentoring. (We talked about informal and formal mentoring in the previous chapter.) Most initial mentorships will begin somewhere along a range of relationship depths in between the two extremes (e.g., "mere acquaintance" and others). You should note that much of this chapter's content is aimed at mentors faced with situations closer to the "stranger" and "mere acquaintance" half of the continuum. The reason is that many unpleasant but completely avoidable incidents occur in these situations, and they happen even to experienced mentors. If you do not face such a situation, you may zoom in only on the sections of the chapter that are relevant to you.

Mentorship Building: Two Key Practices

Before we discuss goal-refining, let's talk about mentorship building. Mentors should first recognize that a mentorship is basically a relationship. Indeed, a good mentorship is in many ways like a good relationship. As you will agree, good relationships don't just happen overnight. You have to invest time and energy to build the relationship and to maintain it. Because we are now talking about the Establishing phase, we are more interested in the building and less in the maintaining. The question, then, is: How do we build? Because a mentorship is a relationship, we can learn from other types of human relationships and use those lessons to build our mentorships.

A great place to start is the human relationship we call "friendship." Think about the strong friendships you now enjoy. Think about how those friendships began, and what you and your friend did to strengthen them.

Social scientists have uncovered a bunch of factors that contribute to friendship-building. We'd like to focus on two only. The first factor is about interacting. People who become friends (PWBFs) frequently bump into each other. These encounters represent opportunities for interaction. But PWBFs do not let such opportunities slip away; they seize them and actually interact. Moreover, they interact frequently.

The second factor is about connecting. PWBFs actively and deliberately seek out common ground in order to connect with each other. (Common ground consists of actual or perceived similarities between two people.) What we call "making small talk" is part of connecting. Connecting entails self-disclosure, which is the revelation of personal and private information. Such information, however, cannot flow only in one direction. For genuine connection to occur, such information must flow both ways. In other words, the receiver of personal and private information is expected to give back by revealing his or her personal and private information. Social scientists call this giving back "reciprocity."

Mentoring experts believe that similar practices can help to build and maintain mentoring relationships. Let's briefly consider each of them.

Interacting

Tammy Allen and her colleagues (2009) think that interactions function as both the spark and the fuel in mentorships. They theorize that the more the mentor and the mentee interact, the more likely they will have quality discussions and feedback, which in turn can produce a quality relationship. For this reason, they recommend physical proximity as a factor for relationship building—the closer the mentor is to the mentee physically, the more likely they will interact frequently. In our view, physical proximity is desirable but not always feasible. We also believe that mentors and mentees can live without it. So we don't think it's a must, but we think it can be helpful. Frequent interaction, on the other hand, is essential. It's hard to see how meaningful progress can be made without frequent-enough interaction, especially during the Establishing phase. Although no hard-and-fast rule governs frequency, we recommend a rule of thumb: Meet frequently during the early stages of the mentorship, perhaps at least once every month. When the relationship is stronger and the mentee is making solid progress, let the frequency taper off to a mutually acceptable level.

Connecting

Mentors and mentees should actively and deliberately seek out some common ground through appropriate self-disclosure. Common ground includes but is not limited to the following:

- Same hometown
- Mutual friends
- Same hobby or interest
- Shared experiences

As implied earlier, common ground helps the mentor and mentee to connect with each other at the beginning of their mentorship. It's something the two can build their relationship on. But before the two can truly connect, both must reveal personal and private information. By disclosing such information, the sender is communicating to the receiver an unspoken but powerful message: "I trust you. I trust you with this information. And I trust you not to use this information against me in any way." As in the case of friendship, the information cannot flow in one direction only (i.e., from mentor to mentee only or from mentee to mentor only). If the information travels only in one direction, it means there isn't enough trust in the relationship. Moreover, when people give you something, they expect something back—the classic quid pro quo. So self-disclosure can help to build and strengthen a mentoring relationship only when it is reciprocated.

What can be shared between the mentor and the mentee is open to debate; for what is private or personal is highly subjective. And with the advent of social media tools like Facebook and Twitter, a situation that is already complicated has become even more so. Young mentees may expect more self-disclosure from the mentor. They see it as an indication of mentor authenticity. We nevertheless counsel circumspection. We recommend selective self-disclosure, broad or deep, only when appropriate. In practical terms, it means this: Think before you speak. If what you plan to say won't help the mentoring relationship, don't say it.

Boundaries

Another basic thing about relationships that we don't normally think or talk about is the existence of boundaries. In the context of our discussion, boundaries are about the acceptable and unacceptable behaviors within a mentoring relationship.

Every person has his or her personal boundaries. You have your boundaries, your mentee has boundaries as well; and they almost always come in sets and not singly. As mentor, you have to be clear about your own set of mentoring-related boundaries. You need to be aware of your mentee's boundaries too. Here are four common boundary-related issues for you to consider:

Are you OK (or not OK) with the following?
- After-work mentoring on business days
- Mentoring on nonbusiness days (e.g., weekends or holidays)
- Phone calls to home
- After-work or nonbusiness-day socializing

And now, three "more complicated" issues:
- Confidentiality issues
  What, if anything, can be revealed to a third party? Under what conditions can it be revealed?

- "Undiscussables" or taboo topics
  What topics (e.g., office politics, emotions at work) are off-limits for you? What topics are off-limits for your mentee?
- Issues pertaining to romance and sex
  If you are involved in a cross-gender mentoring relationship, what is morally correct?

This list of boundaries isn't meant to be comprehensive, it's meant to stimulate your thinking about them. And wherever appropriate, you should discuss them with your mentee.

One last point about boundaries: They are not static and can change as your relationship evolves over time. Generally, a drop in the number of boundaries is an indicator that your relationship has deepened.

Use the tool in Exhibit 5-1 to clarify mentoring issues.

Goal-Refining

Now that we've dealt with the mentoring relationship fundamentals, we can move on to the main event of the Establishing phase: Goal-refining.

Goal-refining isn't a commonly used term. We begin by describing what it is not. Goal refining is definitely not goal-setting. Goal-setting is about creating a goal. In goal-refining, a goal already exists. And what is this goal?

If you will recall, we said in a previous chapter that the mentee is in the driver's seat and must come to the mentor with three things: a tentative goal, a tentative action plan, and a tentative idea about how the mentor can help him or her. Note that we've used the word *tentative* to characterize them, because there's probably room for improvement in all three. This assumption is broadly true. The three are typically works-in-progress and certain aspects about them can be refined further. It is precisely at this point that goal-refining comes in, and it is exactly what it means: It's about refining the three, especially the third one.

Exhibit 5-1: A Worksheet to Work Through Issues in Mentoring

Directions: Use this worksheet to guide a discussion in mentoring to clarify the relationship. Both mentor and mentee should separately answer the questions appearing under the left column below. They should take notes in the right colum. They should then come together in a meeting to discuss these questions to build the quality of their relationship.

Questions		Answers
1	What should be the focus of our mentoring relationship?	
2	What topics, if any, should be off-limits?	
3	What measurable goals should we establish for our mentoring relationship?	
4	How do we connect? What do we share in common? What are our major differences?	
5	How should we interact? Face-to-face? By phone? By social media such as Twitter? Are there, or should there be, any preferred ways to interact?	
6	What boundaries should we establish in our relationship? For instance, are there times when we should not communicate? Should we communicate at work, outside of work, or both?	

(continued)

	Questions	Answers
7	Should we consider our conversations confidential or not? What topics or issues, if any, should be confidential?	
8	What topics, if any, should be considered undiscussable? For instance, what about office politics? Rumors?	
9	What boundaries, if any, should be placed on possible romantic relationships between us?	
10	What other issues, if any, should be discussed about our relationship?	

Why focus on the third? This item—how the mentee thinks the mentor can help him or her—will *evolve* into the goal of the mentorship. Let's think about this for a moment because it's important. If your mentee says to you, "I think you can help me this way," and you reply, "Yes, I think so too," the two of you will have achieved agreement. If there's no agreement, you cannot move forward together. Hence, agreement represents the starting point of goal-refining. The next step involves a closer look at the tentative action plan and the first item, the *overarching goal*. The two of you then discuss and negotiate and come up with a mutually agreed-upon goal for the mentorship.

You may have noticed that we used the phrase *overarching goal* to describe the first item. Using a distinct term seems to suggest that the overarching goal and the mentorship goal can be different. If you think this, you're absolutely correct. At times, of course, the overarching goal and the mentorship goal will be one and the same, but not always. For example, the first item could be the mentee's long-term, overarching goal and the third item merely a step toward that goal. The following story illustrates the potential difference:

A graduate student approaches her professor, who is also her advisor, with her long-term goal, "I want to become the chief learning officer (CLO) of a global technology firm in fifteen years' time." She then presents to him a fifteen-year plan that can be broken down neatly into three five-year plans. She explains, "The way I see it, I should be in a lower management position in five years' time, a middle management position in ten years' time, and the CLO position by the end of the fifteenth year."

After a few rounds of question-and-answer between the two, the professor responds, "Everything looks good on paper. Is there anything I can do to help you with your plan?"

"Yes, and thank you, I'm glad you asked. I'm looking for three suitable mentors. I'd be grateful if you could please help me find one who's now in a lower management job, one who's now in a middle management job, and one who's now a CLO. The reason I need the three different mentors is because I feel I need to know what work and life are really like at their respective level. Their insights will help me prepare, and, for all you know, they may even change me."

"OK. I'll see what can be done," answers the professor.

"One more thing, Prof. I know that I must be the captain of my life. But I also realize that a sensible captain acknowledges she can't handle life alone and will go get good help. So I was hoping you would be my navigator and sounding board. In other words, my fourth mentor."

The professor ponders the request for a few moments. He likes the self-responsible approach of his prospective mentee and eventually agrees.

As you can see from the story, the graduate student has an obvious long-term goal and a less obvious short-term goal. The long-term goal is, of course, the mentee's CLO dream. The short-term goal is that the professor has agreed to tap into his presumably extensive network of contacts and recommend three appropriate mentors to the mentee. We call it a short-term (by "short-term" we mean a timeframe of two years or less) goal because the mentee will want to see progress and results within a reasonable space of time. The need to see timely progress is true also of the mentorship goal. Without meaningful progress or results in the near term, not many individuals—and we're referring to both mentees and mentors—will want to extend the mentorship. Hence, the relationship has to first make sense to both partners in the short term in order for it to have any chance of becoming a long-term one. At the same time, the professor's short-term goal is most likely to be one among several other short-term goals for that particular mentorship. The point here is that different goals and different kinds of goals can be at work within a single mentorship, and the mentor should have a clear understanding of all of them. (We will talk more about this later in the chapter.)

So, how will goal-refining help the mentee? In a nutshell, it can help the mentee reach his or her goals more efficiently. By refining the three tentative items, the mentor helps the mentee save time and energy in pursuit of a goal. Generally, the mentor's contribution comes in two forms:

- *Goal-relevant knowledge:* The mentor knows things that the mentee doesn't.
- *Goal-relevant questions:* The mentor asks questions that the mentee hasn't considered.

In the next section, we will consider the nitty-gritty of goal-refining.

How to Refine Goals

Earlier, we mentioned that the mentor should "understand" the mentee's goals and know what the mentee's needs or concerns are. This objective is in line with the popular adage, "Seek first to understand." And the best way to understand is to listen.

Listening

Goal-refining begins with listening. How well you listen for the first several sessions may just determine how well your mentoring relationship ends. Much has been written about listening. Yet many people, including mentors, are still getting it wrong and not listening right. Here's a true story about an individual's frustrating experience to illustrate our point:

I needed to learn something about exporting that was new to me and important to my work. So I talked with several people about my question. They all told me that Simon would be the best person to help me with my question and that I should talk with Simon. They also assured me that Simon was an approachable fellow and was usually a helpful person.

Now I knew who Simon was. And I knew what he was famous for or good at. But I had no idea he was also good at the area I was interested in. That was a pleasant surprise. Anyhow, I asked one of my friends to set up a meeting for me with Simon. After a couple of days, my friend said Simon would be more than happy to meet me.

I went to meet Simon as planned. But after the usual pleasantries and small talk, the meeting immediately went south. He kept on talking about what he was famous for. He never once asked me why I was there to see him. Nor did he really give me a chance to clarify my intentions. He dominated the entire conversation. He assumed he knew exactly why I was paying him a visit.

You can just imagine how frustrating this situation must have been for the *almost* mentee. You should also note that this particular mentee is actually a man in his fifties and is himself a veteran mentor. So you shouldn't treat what he described lightly. In other words, we should all listen and learn from the episode.

In this chapter, we won't be going deep into the behavioral aspects of good listening. In other words, we won't be talking much about things like making eye contact, avoiding distracting behaviors, not interrupting, and so on. It's not that they're not important. It's just that plenty of good resources are readily available on the Internet and in the marketplace.

What we're going to address here are the principles of mentoring-related listening. And we put forward to you the two important ones:

- Listening with respect
- Listening to serve

You have already seen the first principle in action (see Chapter 3, The Willingness Factor), so we won't belabor it here. We'll just summarize the principle this way: By listening with respect, you are signaling to the mentee that he or she is worth listening to. You are also helping to create a psychologically safe environment where truly productive mentoring can take place.

The second principle, listening to serve, is to listen with an attitude of service. The attitude component is critically important. Recall that the core purpose of mentoring is to aim for the mentee's growth and to make it happen. At the same time, every mentee is unique and not every growth-related goal is likely to be the same. As mentor, you would do well to assume nothing. So at the outset of the mentorship, you must determine how your mentee wants to grow and how you can help make that growth happen (i.e., your service).

To determine the mentee's growth needs, you can use the first two of the three items that we talked about earlier. They are the tentative goal and the tentative action plan. Turn them into the following questions:

- What do you hope to accomplish?
- How will you accomplish it?

Indeed, questioning is part of listening—they go hand in hand. The mentor shouldn't shy away from questions. Use them wisely and you will reap great rewards.

To determine how you can serve your mentee, turn the third and final item into a question as well. A simple yet effective "How can I help you?" (or one of its equivalents, for example, "What can I do to help you") should do it. In the story of Simon and our friend, Simon failed to listen with respect and listen to serve. Hence, it doesn't surprise us that the meeting "went south."

At the end of the day, listening allows you to customize your enablement regimen, because your mentee is unique and a one-size-fits-all regimen doesn't exist. When you listen and understand and customize, your regimen will be data-driven and not arbitrary. Furthermore, by listening, you are signaling to your mentee that he or she is worthy of your attention and that you value him or her. The mentee will think: "My mentor cares about me. I can trust my mentor."

The Mentorship Goal

Let's suppose that you've fully understood the mentee's goals and plans, and that you're certain you're able to help him or her. The next step, then, is to actually refine the third item, the mentorship goal. How do we do that? "Use SMART" is one highly probable answer. SMART, as many of you might know, is a famous and popular goal-related acronym. Many of today's managers have been conditioned to think that SMART is the solution to every goal-related problem.

The problem is the numerous versions of SMART. If you visit the online encyclopedia, Wikipedia, and look up the entry "SMART criteria," you will discover a wide array of possible SMARTs. Take the letter S, for example. S can mean "specific," "significant," "stretching," or "simple." In other words, there is no consensus.

Perhaps it's best that we step back and remind ourselves what SMART truly is. It is basically an acronym. Acronyms, for the most part, are mnemonic devices that help us remember things, not solve problems. Nevertheless, since SMART is the dominant logic in goal-related matters, we will use it—but not 100 percent in the conventional way. For us, SMAART is more appropriate than SMART. SMAART stands for:

- **Specific:** The goal is clearly articulated—when he or she reaches it, the goal pursuer will know for certain that he or she has truly arrived.
- **Measurable:** The goal is, to a large extent, quantifiable.
- **Agreed:** Both mentee and mentor agree that the goal is worth pursuing.
- **Action-oriented:** Using action verbs, the goal pursuer outlines the exact steps to be taken to accomplish the goal.
- **Realistic:** The goal is a mission probable.
- **Time-bound:** A deadline must be met.

As you can see, the components, specific, measurable and time-bound, are conventional and won't raise too many eyebrows. Furthermore, these three components have time and again proven their effectiveness in the refining of short-term goals. The two A and R components are, however, slightly more controversial. We chose these particular components mainly because the mentorship goal is a short-term goal, and short-terms goals demand action and need to be realistic.

Use these components as criteria to refine your mentee's short-term goals and everything should be OK. For example, the goal "my mentee wants to sell one LED3D television every business week throughout 2011" can be a SMAART goal. First, it satisfies the S, M, and T components. Second, the mentor has to decide whether it is a worthy goal, which can be easily determined. However, whether the goal is sufficiently action-oriented and realistic is context-dependent and represents a judgment call. Here, the mentor will have to rely on his or her wisdom and experience.

The Long-Term, Overarching Goal

When refining your mentee's short-term goal, the mentor has to ask the question, "Does the short-term goal make sense in the overall scheme of things?"

To answer this question, the mentor considers the long-term, over-arching goal. Such goals may appear unrealistic to the mentor, especially when the mentee who came up with the goal is at his or her early career stage. You may think to yourself, "Can he or she do it?" Despite your reservations, don't discourage your young mentee. Focus instead on the plausibility of the long-term goal. Even here, we urge you to take a leap of faith with your mentee into the realm of possibilities. In other words, be supportive and suspend your judgment for the time being. If both the short and the long appear coherent and logically sound, then assume that the short-term goal makes sense. The point is that being overly realistic may not be such a good thing for the mentee's dreams. However, as time passes and you've grown to know your mentee much better, if you see the goal has become unrealistic or a lack of potential or ability becomes apparent, you will have to give honest feedback to him or her.

CHAPTER 6

THE REFLECTIVE MENTOR

"The unexamined life is not worth living."
—Socrates, Greek philosopher

Experience Is the Best Teacher

Many of us are familiar with the old saw "Experience is the best teacher," and many of us would agree. But how can we, as individuals, learn from experience?

One old and time-tested way is reflection.

Reflection—now that's another familiar thing, and it seems to be a big deal too. It's been said that reflection is "an art of which *every* man [and woman] should be a master." Yet questions abound:

- What exactly is reflection?
- How do we reflect? Even if we do reflect, are we reflecting effectively?
- How is reflection relevant to mentoring?

In this chapter, we will answer these questions, and more. Specifically, we will define reflection, explain why it is important to you and your mentee (and, therefore, why reflection is a core mentoring skill), and show you how to reflect effectively. At the end of the chapter, we include a section—a brief overview and preview—on how to use what you've learned from your reflections to benefit your mentee.

Reflection Explained

Reflection is a process that enables an *individual* mentor to extract *learning* from his or her *past experiences*. It is a thinking-intensive process, but one that can be performed systematically. Because this book is about mentoring, our definition shows a discernible bias toward mentoring. At the same time, it contains three words or phrases (in italics) that require our close attention. We will further develop most of them in the other sections, but for now, we will look at them briefly (and not in the order in which they appear).

Individual

For the purposes of this chapter, we focus on the individual practice of reflection, which is more commonly referred to as self-reflection. Nevertheless, we readily acknowledge that reflection can also be a group practice. If you have participated in an "after-action review," "lessons-learned session," "postmortem," or anything similar at the workplace, you will have already practiced group reflection.

Past Experiences

Buried inside every mentor's past are nuggets of wisdom, knowledge, and understanding. Some are in fact buried so deep you may not even be aware of their existence. The main point is this: If they remain buried, they are of no value to you as a mentor or to your mentee. The reasonable thing to do then is to take them out; and the extractive technology is reflection, so to speak.

Learning

Learning is the most important word in our definition. It is, however, a word that can mean different things to different people, so it behooves us to clarify what we mean by it. Here, learning can mean one of two things:

- Isolating thought(s) or behavior(s) that are beneficial to the mentor, or
- Isolating change(s) in thought or behavior that are beneficial to the mentor.

Let's take a closer look at these definitions within our definition.

First, let's deal with the words *behavior* and *thought*. Everything that is outwardly observable is considered as behavior. It encompasses the mentor's actions and interactions with the people around him or her. It includes a mentor's words, deeds, and even body language. *Thought* refers to the thinking (e.g., assumption, perspective) behind a specific behavior. It goes without saying that thought is not outwardly observable, and the notion that thought requires extracting makes intuitive sense. But why does behavior, something that's open for all to see, need extracting? The problem with behaviors is that we sometimes "do" them without consciously thinking about them. Because we don't always think about them, we don't always "see" them, so we can be unaware of or unclear about them—hence, the need for extraction through reflection.

Second, anything (done legally and ethically) that consistently brings success to the mentor is considered beneficial. It means that the isolated thought or behavior has brought success to the mentor not once, not twice, but many times, both in the past and in the present.

Finally, "isolating" means separating by way of examining; that is, the mentor examines his or her thoughts and behaviors and then separates the beneficial ones from the unhelpful ones. Let's face it, nobody's perfect—including mentors—and you can find in every individual both productive and unproductive thoughts and behaviors. They of course produce different results: productive thoughts and behaviors tend to lead to success; unproductive ones lead away from success. Isolating is important because it helps the mentor identify the factors (i.e., thoughts and behaviors) behind his or her current success. By doing so, he or she will have a good idea about what to replicate in the hopes of attaining future and continued success.

We are acutely aware of the possibility that what worked in the past or present may not work in future. Nevertheless, most situations are generic in nature and truly unique situations are rare, so the mentor has a fair chance of succeeding if he or she relies on the tried-and-true. For those situations that may be unique to a mentor but not to other people, a mentor can seek help from those people who have had experience in dealing with situations similar to the one he or she faces. Because there is always room for improvement, the mentor may also choose to work on what's already working, that is, to think and to behave better. Last but not least, isolating helps the mentor to identify the factors behind his or her failures so that he or she can eliminate or mitigate them.

As you can see, the learning produced by reflection is beneficial to you, the mentor. To recap, reflection helps the mentor to surface unconscious thoughts or behaviors to the conscious level. Once they've reached that level, they can be scrutinized. The mentor can then decide what to retain, improve upon, or get rid of.

Reflection is also beneficial to your mentee, the prime beneficiary in any mentoring relationship. It is beneficial to the mentee for the same reasons it is beneficial to the mentor; therefore, we encourage every mentor to teach his or her mentee to self-reflect. Learning the right things from you is another mentee benefit. When you've got a clear understanding about why you're currently successful, you can transmit those success insights to your mentee. Imagine the opposite: Your mentee could be learning all the wrong things if you haven't clearly identified your beneficial thoughts or behaviors. In short, reflection helps you to teach right so your mentee will learn right.

The 4-Step Process

Even though it is a core mentoring skill, reflection isn't necessarily something that people are excited about doing. In this day and age where the dominant mantra seems to be "fire, ready, aim," people feel pressured to act fast or to act continuously. To many, slowing down to reflect seems like a luxury. In addition, people don't do what they don't know. Perhaps the lack of enthusiasm for reflection is because people actually don't know how to reflect.

Taking all the impediments into account, we have developed a reflection process or method that is easy to learn and will help you to reflect effectively. It consists of four steps, and they make up the system that guides your thinking and behavior during reflection. The first step is about deliberately creating or searching for conditions that stimulate reflection. The second step is about selecting the right event to reflect on. The third step is about the reflection proper. The process is driven by a set of simple yet powerful questions, and its objective is to produce learning. Finally, the fourth step is about using the learning. If the learning isn't utilized, our reflection will have been a waste. Let us now look closely at each of the four steps.

Step 1: Get into the Right State

As mentioned earlier, reflection does not happen naturally. Before it can happen, you've got to get yourself into a reflective state or mood. One way to do that is to choose or create an environment that is conducive to reflection. What constitutes conduciveness, however, is subjective. Here, the wisdom of "different strokes for different folks" applies. Nevertheless, we offer some general suggestions:

- Designate a specific day (e.g. every Saturday or Sunday) or a specific time (e.g., early mornings or moments before you go to bed) as "reflection time." *Note: Some of you may know of mentors who reflect daily and wonder whether we are underprescribing reflection. We are not, and we'd like to clarify that their daily reflections are different from what we are discussing here. For those who reflect daily, they are going back over their day, perhaps asking themselves, "How did I do today?" Our version of "reflection time," on the other hand, is meant for key events—events that are especially meaningful to the reflecting individual—and they do not happen every day. (We will further develop the idea of "key events" in Step 2.)*

- Find a place that gets you into a positive, contemplative mood.
- Make yourself comfortable. Wear something comfortable. Use reflection-friendly furniture. Pay attention also to ambient factors such as lighting and room temperature. Additionally, if you find certain music and aromas helpful, use them.
- Allow no interruptions (e.g., turn off your cell phone).

The bottom line: Do whatever gets you into a positive, contemplative mood.

Step 2: Focus on the Right Event

We mentioned in Step 1 that reflection involves the recall of a *key event*, and we wish to elaborate on this concept here. Both *key* and *event* are important words. We will look first at *event*, and then *key*.

The Definition of *Event*. An event is a past episode of your life (which includes work-related experiences) during which you endeavored to accomplish a short-term SMART 1.0 goal. (See the previous chapter for a refresher on SMART 1.0.) The event should have a clear start date and a clear end date, both of which correspond to the "time-bound" component, or T in the SMART mnemonic. It contains actions, which corresponds to the A or "action-oriented" component. And both the S ("specific") and M ("measurable") components tell you in clear terms whether you've accomplished what you set out to do.

You can use the components to differentiate or isolate one event from another. To illustrate, here are a couple of examples:

- *Example 1*: Your success in sealing a $10 million deal with XYZ, Inc., in 2009 is an event. Your success in sealing a $15 million deal with XYZ, Inc., in 2010 is another. Reason: Different year (the "T" in SMART); therefore different events.
- *Example 2*: Your success in sealing a $10 million deal with XYZ, Inc., in 2009 is an event. Your success in sealing a $20 million deal with ABC, Inc., in 2009 is another. Reason: Different "S" and "M"; therefore different events.

Event Selection Criterion 1: The "Key" in "Key Event." Because it is possible to differentiate between events, it is possible for us to isolate an event for reflection. That's what Step 2 is about. Not every goal-pursuit of yours is reflection-worthy, however. You should focus only on "key" events. The problem is that we pursue multiple SMART 1.0 goals year in and year out. Which ones would qualify as "key"? As mentioned earlier, a key event is one that you find meaningful. The dictionary defines meaningful as "serious, important, or useful." Therefore, key events are those that involve important SMART goals—goals that are important to you and probably to your organization as well. In addition, the emotional content of an event is usually a good indicator of meaningfulness. Key events tend to be highly emotional. If an event hits you in the heart or gut, it's likely to be a key one.

Event Selection Criterion 2: Recency. It's also good to reflect on a key event that is still fresh in your mind. Because recent events are generally fresher than those farther back in the past, you will want to take into account an event's recency when selecting events for reflection. Recency is also a factor in that the details (i.e., facts, thoughts, and emotions) of an event are important, and you will want to recall as many of them as possible. (You shall see later why they are necessary.) You should be able to remember the details of recent events well; the details of older events, on the other hand, are normally harder to recall. Additionally, players involved in a recent event are most probably still contactable, which allows you to perform cross-checking if the need arises. In contrast, you may have difficulty contacting players of older events; some of them may have retired or left the organization.

Performing Step 2. Think about all the events you can still remember and select one which fulfills the twin criteria of meaningfulness and recency. By limiting it to only one key event per reflection time, you will help your mind to focus.

The Reflection Journal. Before we move on to Step 3, we must first address the critical subject of capturing your learning and the details. Reflection is mainly about learning, and much of that takes place in your mind. If it stays there, its usefulness will be severely limited, first of all because you won't be able to transmit your learning easily to your mentee, because it's all literally in your head. You have to somehow get it out in the open, either in words (oral or written) or in deeds. Secondly, your memory, your brain's storage system, isn't perfect and some of your learning could get lost; in some instances, the losses are permanent. Therefore, to improve retention, you must capture your learning. Finally, it is much easier for us to examine something that is visible and explicit, which is especially helpful when we must closely examine our own learning in order to grow and develop.

As you reflect, the details surrounding the key event will emerge. Do not ignore them. The details are important, as mentioned earlier, so you will want to capture them. The bottom line: Your learning and details of the event must be captured in some shape or form.

For capturing both the details and your learning, we recommend the good old-fashioned journal. When we record facts, thoughts, or emotions, some of us prefer to use words, while others prefer visuals. Journals are great in that they allow the composition of texts and free-hand drawings. With both verbal and visual modes of communication at your disposal, you should be able to capture as many of the details surrounding a key event as possible. The two modes can of course be used in combination.

Also, do not worry about what or how you capture. Just scribble what comes to mind. Do not self-censor. And do not edit. The reason for letting yourself go is to allow your journal to function as a true instrument of reflection. Your entries must not be too planned or too guarded, especially when they are meant for your personal consumption only. If security is a concern, consider putting your journal under lock and key. Consider using the format that appears in Exhibit 6-1 for your reflection journal.

Step 3: Ask the Right Questions

Someone once said that "the ability to ask the right question is more than half the battle of finding the answer." We agree, and we have developed some terrific questions for you.

Exhibit 6-1: A Sample Format for a Reflection Journal

Directions: A reflection journal does not have to be formalized. Keeping it simple is preferable to something fancy. As noted in the chapter, do not worry about what or how you capture. Just scribble what comes to mind. Do not self-censor. And do not edit.

Ideas/Point of Reflection	Keep Points to Share

Level 1 Questions. Level 1 questions are based on the fact that every key event involves a SMART goal and they help us to determine whether that goal is achieved.

To get started, use the following Level 1 questions sequentially:

- Question 1.1: What did I set out to accomplish?
- Question 1.2: What did I actually accomplish?
- Question 1.3: Are my answers to Questions 1 and 2 different?

If your response to Question 1.3 is "Yes, they are different," proceed to Level 2. However, if your answer to Question 1.3 is "No, they are *not* different," you should be congratulated for your impeccable planning and execution. Complete your reflection by pulling out the key learning points with Question 1.4: "What did I do right?" If you find that you did many right things, condense your learning with Question 1.4.1: "What three things were essential for my success?"

A useful supplementary question is Question 1.5: "Can I do the right thing(s) faster, better, and/or cheaper the next time I face a situation with a similar SMART goal?" Your response can lead to future refinements to your actions.

Level 2 Questions. Level 2 questions help us to uncover the reasons behind the discrepancy and to formulate a response that is likely to prevent the recurrence of the discrepancy.

It is important to note that two types of discrepancies are possible:

- Positive discrepancy: You accomplished *more* than what you set out to accomplish.
- Negative discrepancy: You accomplished *less* than what you set out to accomplish.

Both types of discrepancy require your attention, especially if you are in a profession with practically zero tolerance for deviation (e.g., military, nuclear power). However, if what you actually accomplished is within the ballpark number of your target (within a zone of tolerance, if you will), you may choose to ignore the discrepancy, whether positive or negative.

A BRIEF NOTE ON POSITIVE DISCREPANCIES

It makes intuitive sense to look closer at a negative discrepancy. But you may be scratching your head, wondering, "Why on earth do I need to pay attention to a positive discrepancy?"

Indeed, a positive discrepancy is often a pleasant experience, which leads to a tendency to leave it at that. But doing so will deprive you of a learning opportunity. Instead, you should dig deeper and ask yourself some tough questions.

Typically, a discrepancy occurs when things don't go according to plan. The same principle applies to positive discrepancies. Something changed, something unexpected happened, and it altered the final results. Whenever a change is about to occur, you will often notice signals. Some of these signals are strong, but some of them weak. The strong ones are easy to detect. The weak ones are more elusive.

Ask yourself:

- Why did you not see it coming?
- If you were more open-minded, or if you had looked harder and smarter, could you (and would you) have seen it?

The Level 2 questions can be broken down into three sublevels, namely 2.1, 2.2, and 2.3.

Level 2.1 Questions. The objective of Level 2.1 is to describe the key event more fully. Level 2.1 questions consist of Who, What, Where, When and Which questions. Here are some examples:

- What happened?
- When did it happen?
- Where did it happen?
- Who was involved?
- What was my involvement?
- Which piece of equipment was involved?

If the key event is protracted and/or complex, you can use a non-question aid to help you rewind the event in your mind. Use the timeline of the event and break it down into three stages: the beginning, the middle, and the end. Then break every stage down into "mini episodes."

Level 2.2 Questions. The objective of Level 2.2 is to analyze the discrepancy deeply (and *not* to assign blame). Use Why questions at this Level. We recommend the "Five Whys" method made popular by the Japanese. Begin with the question, "Why was there a discrepancy?" Answer it in the following format, "Because such-and-such happened." Then question your answer, "Why did such-and-such happen?" Repeat the same line of questioning until you are satisfied you have reached the root cause of the discrepancy. Experience suggests that it takes about five whys to get to the bottom of things. So don't give up too early.

In all likelihood, the answers generated at Level 2.1 can help you answer some of the Level 2.2 Why questions. Additionally, you could ask, "What else entered into the event and had an impact on the outcome?" Most important, be truthful. You may not like some of the answers, but nothing will get better unless you face the truth.

Level 2.3 Questions. You should have gathered sufficient data by now to generate potential solutions, which is precisely what Level 2.3 is about. Here, How questions are especially useful. The following is an example: "What actions might I take so that the discrepancy won't happen again?" or more simply, "How might I do things differently?"

Another useful How question is this one: "How is this event similar to (or different from) other events?" This one helps us to make connections with other events and to learn and draw potential solutions from them.

The question levels and focus of each level are summarized in Exhibit 6-2.

Step 4: Decide the Right Thing

Step 4 is about using the learning generated by your self-reflection. The question is: How do we do that? In a word, you need to decide. Deciding is always part and parcel of using the information generated from reflection. If you will recall, you were asked at several points during Step 3 to come up with potential replications, refinements, or solutions. Chances are, you came up with more than one (regardless of the situation you face), meaning you have choices. And when faced with

Exhibit 6-2: Asking the Right Questions

Type of Question	Question Focus	Examples of Questions
Level 1 Questions	Goals and goal achievement	• What did I set out to accomplish? • What did I actually accomplish? • Are my answers to questions 1 and 2 different?
Level 2 Questions	Reasons behind discrepancies and ways to prevent the recurrence of discrepancies	
Level 2.1 Questions	Describes events more fully	• What happened? • When did it happen? • Where did it happen? • Who was involved? • What was my involvement? • Which piece of equipment was involved?
Level 2.2 Questions	Analyzes discrepancies deeply (but does not assign blame)	• Why did it happen? • Use the 5 Whys technique
Level 2.3 Questions	Generates solutions	• How can the discrepancy be addressed?

choices, you have to decide. Specifically, you need to make a decision on one or more of the following:

- Level 1, Questions 1.4 and 1.4.1: What should you replicate in the future?
- Level 1, Question 1.5: What should you refine and how should you refine it (or them)?
- Level 2, Question 2.3: What should you stop doing? And what should you do next?

Here are several principles that will help you decide better:

- If you can afford not to rush into a decision, don't rush. Take as much time as allowed, even if it means going beyond your reflection time. (Yes, Step 4 can be long.)
- Before you decide on something . . .
  - Know the principles or values that guide your decision making.
  - Know what success looks like to you and other key stakeholders.
  - Know that potential solutions or refinements rarely emerge robust or workable, so spend time and effort to improve them.
  - Consider the time and resources required to make your solution or refinement work.
  - Know that every decision has implications or consequences; identify them and think through them.
  - Remember that two heads are often better than one; consult your mentor (yes, mentors can have mentors) if you need input.
- Action is not a necessary outcome of every decision-making process. Inaction (albeit temporary) can be a perfectly legitimate decision in certain situations (e.g., wait-and-see).
- We are imperfect beings—and our decisions are likewise imperfect—but don't let your imperfection paralyze you into indecision.

Once you've made a decision, commit to it. Give it your best shot. Persevere.

Reflect after some time to determine whether your decision (replication, solution, or refinement) works. If mistakes do occur, learn from them. When you do that, they are no longer mistakes; they've become "lessons."

Teach the Right Things, and Teach Them Right

Everything you do in a mentoring relationship must ultimately benefit your mentee, and earlier in this chapter we suggested that your mentee will ultimately benefit from your reflection. That is, when you know what makes you successful, you can then teach it to your mentee. These lessons are obviously important for your mentee, so you've got to do two things: Teach the right things, and teach them right.

Teaching the Right Things

We've already discussed "the right thing" earlier (see "Learning" under "Reflection Explained"), so we'll just summarize and emphasize a few things here.

First, the right thing is legal and ethical. You have no qualms about doing it. And it's not going to give you, your mentee, or your company any bad trouble down the road.

Second, the right thing is effective. It's something that has consistently brought you success. It's not based on hearsay. It's been tested by experience—yours. You're confident that it works, and you will not hesitate to use it again and again (until something or someone tells you it's no longer working).

Finally, the right thing is not the product of a one-time reflection. Rather, it is the product of many reflections taking place over a number of years. The right thing is the mentor's cumulative learning.

What are some of the right things? Recall that the right things can be thought-based or behavioral. Let us first consider the behavioral aspect. Anecdotal evidence suggests that the most common behaviors that mentees learn from mentors are efficiency-related. They are about helping the mentee reach his or her goal faster, cheaper, or relatively painlessly. They are also about doing work in a better way. Your mentee achieves this by:

- Using the beneficial habits, shortcuts, or enhancements that you recommend or exemplify.
- Avoiding the mistakes or pitfalls that you highlight.

Behavior is all about action and interaction. In contrast, thoughts are mainly concerned with attitude (or perspective, or perception). In order to succeed, what attitude should your mentee adopt toward life in general and difficult situations in particular? You must realize that thoughts can and do guide behaviors. And when your mentee's thoughts aren't productive and are leading to unproductive behaviors, you should help reframe them.

Adopting from Others

We've so far touched upon the right things that you generate through self-reflection. The next question is: Is it OK to adopt "the right things" generated by others? (Sources that qualify as "others" include your mentor, your education, and your training.) The answer is, of course, yes. But we add this: "Do not adopt blindly!" You should, in fact, reflect before you adopt. But in this case, you need not go through the whole Four Steps. Here, a highly abbreviated version will suffice.

First, you must realize that nothing happens in a vacuum. You should therefore always consider the context. Ask yourself: "What is the context in which the other-generated (as opposed to self-generated) right thing was generated?" Once that context has been adequately described, ask yourself another question: "How similar (or different) is that context to the situation I am in?" If you're convinced that the other situation and your situation are similar enough, you can proceed with the adoption.

Here's another recommendation: Test your adoption. That is, you should test your adoption just the way you test your self-generated right thing. The key yardstick remains the same: Your adoption must consistently produce success for you in a legal and ethical way.

Now, the final recommendation: You need not adopt wholesale. If you find certain parts of the other person's right thing somewhat iffy or downright wrong, you need not adopt those parts. But don't throw the baby out with the bathwater. Adopt what is good, reject what is bad.

Packaging Your Content

You have content, but there's a problem: It isn't always easily transmittable. For example, thoughts are abstract and invisible, so how does the mentor transmit something that has those qualities? One possible solution: The mentor can articulate his or her thoughts verbally or in writing. We call all such solutions "content packaging."

Content can be packaged in many different ways. We strongly recommend two: mentoring stories and the Success Manual.

Mentoring Stories. Mentoring stories are important enough to warrant their own chapter (see Chapter 8, The Storytelling Mentor). For this reason, we will only briefly develop the subject here.

The first thing about mentoring stories is that they're versatile and can be used to enable or uplift. In other words, stories are a great teaching tool, but they don't have to be used exclusively for teaching purposes. Your reflection journal is a key source of raw materials that can be packaged into full-blown stories. For example, mentoring stories, like any good story, contain both facts and feelings (emotions), and you can get all these from your journal. (And now you know why we asked you to record the facts, thoughts, and emotions surrounding key events in a no-holds-barred sort of way.)

The Success Manual. The Success Manual is a booklet that contains your personal success recipes. And like mentoring stories, it is a teaching tool. How you write your individual recipe depends on what your recipe is about. If it's about a relatively straightforward task (i.e., one that does not involve many steps and can be completed within a workweek or even a workday, for example, cooking a dish, performing a medical procedure, writing a business letter), you can then write it in a cookbook style, that is, each recipe should contain clear and sufficiently detailed instructions for performing the task in question. For those of you who work in a mature organization where standard operating procedures (SOPs) or their equivalents are available and accessible, you may ask, "Why reinvent the wheel?" It's a good question, but here is the reason why: the recipes in your Success Manual are actually deviations from the standard. They include shortcuts and other sorts of enhancements, and they must be beneficial (and legal and ethical). So your Success Manual isn't meant to replace your company's SOPs; rather, it is meant to supplement them.

If you're writing about a task that's complicated (i.e., one that involves many steps, many people, and many weeks, for example, negotiating a big deal or resolving a major conflict), you will have to write your recipe in a different way. In such a situation, a case (as in case study) style would be most appropriate. You are not expected to write something as elaborate as a graduate school case but you will have to produce something that is case-like. Think of a case as a story, which it is. It is a story about you, the mentor, solving a real problem or dealing with a real situation. And it's a story that is meant to be read, not told. Some mentors are uncomfortable with case-writing, so we're making it an option. Those who have chosen to do it have found it to be an illuminating experience.

Your Success Manual can of course have an assortment of cookbook-style recipes, models, and cases in it. In both recipes and cases, you should also reveal your thinking behind your behaviors. You can think of the rationales as your responses to the question "Why are you doing this?" You should be able to get much of the "raw material" from your reflection journal.

As mentioned earlier, the Success Manual is a teaching tool, so it's meant to help you teach better. Remember: You're teaching thoughts and behaviors. Behaviors are observable and concrete and from a mentee standpoint more absorbable. In other words, behaviors are easier to teach. Thoughts on the other hand are invisible. But by putting your thoughts on paper you're making something invisible visible, which facilitates its teaching.

You can also learn through the Success Manual. How? When you bare your thoughts, you are actually letting others (e.g., your mentee or mentor) understand what was going on in your head when you did something. One likely consequence of turning yourself into an open book is that others may challenge your thoughts and actions. (You could also invite people to challenge you with a polite and sincere "What do you think?") When a challenge does happen, listen with an open mind. If you have to defend, defend without being defensive. Through these meaningful exchanges, you will learn and grow. Indeed, one of the hallmarks of a great mentor is a commitment to lifelong learning, and in many ways, the Success Manual represents the logbook of the mentor's ongoing journey. The implication is that the contents of the Success Manual may change. In all likelihood, they will, because nothing is set in stone. The Success Manual is a living and evolving document, just as you are a living and evolving human being.

Teaching Right: The Challenge

Getting the content and its packaging right is only half the work. The other half involves using the content and packaging in a correct way. That is what "teaching right" is about.

You must realize by now that teaching is a big part of a mentor's job, so that makes teaching right highly important. You should also realize that teaching is a big challenge in the workplace. To begin with, many managers (the natural candidates for mentors) are not qualified teachers. This reality is not surprising—after all, most managers aren't hired for their teaching abilities. In fact, many managers would be shocked if told that teaching is a part of their everyday work! The limited supply of qualified manager-mentors no doubt creates a problem for mentoring. Even if a manager is interested in teaching, few in the workplace can show him or her how.

Things are beginning to change, however. The biggest is perhaps the change in perception. The idea of managers as teachers is no longer considered strange. On the contrary, it's something very real at today's leading business organizations. Exemplary practitioners include Ken Schroeder, the former CEO of technology firm KLA-Tencor, and Jack

Welch, the former CEO of GE. But the supply of manager-mentors will not expand automatically even though more and more managers accept that they have to teach. As implied earlier, someone has to first teach them how to teach. If this type of training is not done, the practice of workplace teaching and mentoring will continue to be hampered by the general lack of teaching ability among manager-mentors.

The solution to the workplace teaching challenge is therefore obvious: Mentors must be taught how to teach. In the course of our research, we discovered two effective teaching techniques: modeling (teaching by example), and storytelling (teaching through stories). Not only are modeling and storytelling important in teaching, they can also be used for uplifting (e.g., inspiring, motivating, or encouraging). The next two chapters are devoted to the concepts and practices of modeling and storytelling.

CHAPTER 7

MENTORING BY EXAMPLE

"There is no teaching to compare with example."
—Lord Robert Baden-Powell, founder of the Scouting movement

Teaching by Example

Teaching by example, or modeling, is naturally a teaching method. In modeling, the teacher teaches by setting an example, and the student learns by observing the teacher's example and then imitating it.

Modeling has been around for a long time. Several hundred years before the Common Era, the Chinese philosopher Mencius was already an advocate of modeling. Today, modeling is pervasive. Look around you. You are sure to meet many people who have had fruitful modeling experiences. They come from every station and walk of life and they include parents, teachers, leaders, and mentors.

Why has modeling remained so popular for so long? Is its pervasiveness a testament to its efficacy? The short answer is yes. And now, the long answer. First of all, modeling works. Learning occurs and skills (a form of behavior) get transferred from teacher to student. Consider demonstration, a common yet powerful form of teaching by example. Demonstration occurs every day at homes all over the world. A mother shows her son how to cook spaghetti. A father shows his daughter how to play the piano. An aunt shows her favorite nephew how to swim. A grandfather shows his granddaughter how to ride a bicycle. These teaching/learning activities are all demonstrations. They all involve teaching by example. And we all know they can and do produce the desired outcomes. Modeling occurs at the workplace as well. If an organization wants to introduce a specific behavior (e.g., skill) to its workers, it will likely consider one of the various forms of modeling.

But why does modeling work? Imitative learning, the other half of the teaching-by-example equation, may be the reason. Imitative learning basically means learning by observing and copying. It is first of all a universal way of learning; the fact that demonstration (which involves observing and copying) has worked so well across the globe substantiates this point. Second, for many of us, it may be the natural or preferred way to learn. The Greek philosopher Aristotle observed that we start learning this way from the beginning, and this inclination doesn't go away as we get older. "People do what people see," the mentoring expert John Maxwell has famously remarked.

The recently discovered fact that we are hardwired to learn imitatively may explain this inclination of ours. Using sophisticated brain imaging technologies, neuroscientists have shown that our brains contain a type of neurons called "mirror neurons," and these neurons enable us to mimic the actions of another person. In other words, the mirror neurons make it possible for us to learn imitatively. It doesn't require a quantum leap in logic to connect mirror neurons with modeling. Daniel Goleman, author of the influential book *Emotional Intelligence*, writes eloquently about the connection: "Spending time with a living, breathing model of effective behavior provides the perfect stimulation of our mirror neurons, which allow us to directly experience, internalize, and ultimately emulate what we observe" (Goleman and Boyatzis, 2008, p. 80).

To sum up, teaching by example is practiced extensively because it works. And it works because it involves a universal and natural or widely preferred way of learning.

Role Modeling

Teaching is a big part of a mentor's work. Given the effectiveness of modeling, it is no surprise then that mentors have incorporated teaching by example into their repertoire of mentoring methods. Indeed, experts have described modeling as being "central to all types of mentoring" (Liang, Spencer, Brogan, and Corral, 2008, p. 178). But how do mentors practice it, exactly? Based on anecdotal evidence, many mentors seem to practice "role modeling," a distinct variant of modeling (Scandura and Viator, 1994). In role modeling, the mentee still learns by watching the mentor in action. But he or she may be watching from a distance with little or no contact between the two. Because of the minimal contact, role modeling is characterized as "passive."

Can learning result from passive modeling? Absolutely. That's because mirror neurons enable learning in such situations. Consider the "power" of stars—sports stars, movie stars, or others of their ilk. They are role models, and those of us who have children should be familiar with the influence that they have over human behavior. This power can even facilitate the acquisition of new skills. Here's a case in point: a teenage kid in a remote part of Africa can learn to moon-walk just by watching a Michael Jackson video. Yes, no contact with the King of Pop is necessary, which means that passive modeling works.

While most experts agree that passive modeling works, some wonder whether its effectiveness can be further enhanced. They wonder in particular whether zero or minimal contact is actually a good thing, and whether some meaningful interaction or interchange between the mentor and mentee during the modeling process could improve the overall effectiveness of the method. These are great questions. Let's think about them ourselves for a moment. Suppose you have a mentor and you observe him or her doing something. If that something isn't too complex, you won't have any difficulty copying it. But what if that something isn't straightforward? What if you have questions like, "Why on earth did my mentor do that?" In passive modeling your questions will most likely remain unanswered, perhaps forever. In many instances, the mentee may be forced to imitate the mentor's actions blindly or unquestioningly, which surely cannot be a good thing.

Modeling 2.0

We strongly believe that passive modeling can be improved, and we have improved it. We call our improved version Modeling 2.0 and it is the topic for the rest of this chapter.

A Brief Overview of Modeling 2.0

Task competence is a mentee goal common across mentoring relationships, which is not surprising as life (and work) is filled with tasks. Balancing a checkbook, planning a vacation, and conducting market research are all tasks. Modeling 2.0 is a mentoring method that is effective for teaching task competence.

Modeling 2.0 represents a synthesis of the good in modeling. It has retained all the traditional yet effective principles and practices. At the same time, steps have been taken to weed out the dubious passiveness that was described earlier. In other words, Modeling 2.0 is dynamic modeling. By "dynamic," we mean that a meaningful interaction or interchange takes place between the mentor and mentee, and this dynamism is evident throughout the method.

In Modeling 2.0, a mentee is deemed to have attained task competence when he or she is able to perform a particular task in a manner that meets the performance standards relevant to that task. The following true story illustrates this point.

Jane was a young doctor who wanted to become a pediatrician. (In many Commonwealth countries, doctors do not specialize immediately upon graduation.) She approached Doris, a senior pediatrician, for advice. Doris informed Jane that one of the tasks she would have to master was intubation. Intubation is an effective way to deal with serious breathing problems in newborn babies that could result in death if not dealt with immediately.

"You will need to attend a training program first," said Doris. "I will arrange for you to attend one as soon as possible," she added.

Jane attended the training program and learned the theories. She also got to practice intubation on a mannequin. She did well in her training, and Doris was pleased with Jane's evaluation results. Jane then asked when she would get a chance to perform an actual intubation.

"In due time," Doris answered. "This is how it's going to work. First, you will see me do two. Next is the 'test': you will do one with me watching you. If you pass the 'test,' you can then do it on your own. Is this a deal?" she asked. Jane responded in the affirmative.

Their discussion, however, ended with an interesting disclosure from Doris. "You should know this—how I do intubation is different from what you learned during your training. I don't use the stylet [i.e., a gadget commonly used in intubation]. If you will recall, the stylet, when used improperly, can cause damage to the trachea [i.e., the windpipe]." Jane nodded in agreement: she did learn that during training. "I've found a way to intubate without using the stylet. By not using it, we greatly reduce the potential damage to the trachea. I want you to intubate this way." Jane just sat there and smiled intelligently. She didn't really know how to react. But in her mind, she was thinking these thoughts: I can't wait to learn and practice her technique.

The day of the first observation came as planned and, as agreed, Doris modeled intubation for Jane. In addition, she directed Jane's attention to the nonconventional aspects of her technique. After the procedure, they both sat down to reflect on their experience, and whatever questions that Jane had, Doris answered them clearly and patiently. In the second observation, the same things more or less repeated themselves.

The time for Jane's "test" finally arrived. She was naturally a bit nervous. Who could blame her? After all, a wrong move on her part could jeopardize a child's well-being. Sensing her mentee's sudden lack of confidence, Doris offered some encouragement, "Don't worry, you'll do fine. I'm right here beside you." Those few words made a world of difference—they helped Jane to compose herself and everything went without a hitch. Doris congratulated Jane at the end of the procedure. A grateful Jane thanked Doris in return.

In the story, the task in question was the intubation of newborn babies, and the relevant performance standard was that the intubation be performed without the use of a stylet. (There were, of course, other performance standards in the actual situation; but for illustrative purposes, the story focused on just one.) We also read that when Jane initially met Doris, she was far from task competent. Nevertheless, actions were taken to address her situation and at the end of it all, she succeeded in achieving her goal. Implicitly, her success suggests that the actions were effective.

Most of the actions taken are in fact Modeling 2.0 practices. What are they? What are the principles behind them? We shall answer these questions in the next section. But before we do that, you should note that Modeling 2.0 can be divided in two phases: in Phase 1, mentors teach through demonstrating, whereas in Phase 2, mentors encourage mentees to practice while under the mentor's observation and receiving feedback. We begin our discussion with Phase 1.

Phase 1

The key teaching principle in Phase 1 is *teaching by example*, and its opposite is the key learning principle, *learning by observing*. When translated into action, they look roughly like this: The mentor models the execution of a task, and the mentee observes the execution. But translating them into real-world action isn't so straightforward. For one thing, the principles have implications, and in the ensuing discussion, we will describe the actions that the mentor can and should take to address the implications.

To ensure a discussion that is systematic and easy to follow, we have divided Phase 1 into the following three subphases (in chronological terms):

- Phase 1A: Pre-observation
- Phase 1B: Observation
- Phase 1C: Post-observation

We will also make occasional references to the Doris-and-Jane story (with additional revelations) to link our discussion to real-world actions.

Phase 1A: Pre-Observation. Observation has to occur for an unavoidable reason: If the mentee can't observe the mentor, then the mentee can't copy the mentor's behaviors, which is the essence of modeling. The implication is therefore obvious: The mentee has to observe.

The action required should be equally obvious: The mentor must act to ensure that observation does indeed take place. In fact, the mentor should deliberately and systematically create opportunities for it to happen. Much of the planning and action should take place during pre-observation, the period before the actual observation. We will now look at the first Mentor Action in Modeling 2.0: Create "watching opportunities."

Mentor Action 1: Create "Watching Opportunities." A mentor can create "watching opportunities" in several ways. We recommend four, all of which are widely accepted workplace practices:

- Work-shadowing (e.g., attend meetings together, visit clients together)
- The mentor invites the mentee to collaborate on a project
- The mentor provides samples of the mentor's work to the mentee
- The mentee attends events (e.g., conferences, dinners) with the mentor

We are sure other ways to create "watching opportunities" are available, and we encourage you to think expansively and creatively when forming them.

The mentor should also be aware that one-time exposure to the task is often not enough for the mentee. Repeated exposures are often valuable and necessary. You saw an example of this in the Doris-and-Jane story: Jane was required to observe intubation twice.

Consequently, the mentor may have to create multiple "watching opportunities," sometimes more than twice.

Finally, the mentor should constantly be on the lookout for observable teachable moments. When such unplanned opportunities arise, the mentor should seize them and invite the mentee to participate in them.

"Observing Is Much More Than Just Seeing." The mentor must realize something important about observation: Observing is much more than just seeing. Indeed, the great fictional detective Sherlock Holmes once teased his very good friend Dr. Watson, "You see, but you do not observe." Holmes's good-natured banter is an eye-opener. It implies that not everyone is a competent observer. Therefore, the mentor shouldn't assume that his mentee is one. So, in order to learn from modeling, the mentee has to observe sufficiently well. Can he be taught to do that? If yes, then how?

Sherlock Holmes is again generous and has provided us with clues to the answer. In the eyes of the great fictional detective, to observe is to pay attention, sometimes even to seemingly trivial details (which is an action that can break cases). In addition, observation entails not only Holmes's sense of sight, but his other senses (e.g., hearing, smell, taste, or touch) as well. The point for mentors who live in the real world is this: To observe well, the mentee must increase his or her overall awareness. A mentor can do several things to help in this area, and all of them must be done before the actual observation begins. The first one is Mentor Action 2: Assign pre-observation reading.

Mentor Action 2: Assign Pre-Observation Reading. Encourage your mentee to do some pre-observation reading. For example, in the Doris-and-Jane story, Doris could have asked Jane to reread her notes from her intubation training program. (Revelation: She did not do so because little time had passed between the training program and the observation, so she assumed, rightly, that all the important knowledge was still fresh in Jane's mind.) In your case, you could ask your mentee to read the appropriate recipe or case from your Success Manual (see previous chapter) or other reference sources. The mentee may not understand 100 percent of the reading assignment, but it's OK.

By doing the reading assignment, the mentee will at least know what to expect to observe later on (i.e., heightened awareness). If no reading material is available, the mentor must at least describe (verbally or otherwise) the steps in which the task will be accomplished.

Mentor Action 3: Create a Safe Learning Environment. Through the pre-observation reading, your mentee will have gained at least some theoretical knowledge (as opposed to practical experience) about the task in question, which can later help in practice. Also, as mentioned, the mentee is not expected to understand 100 percent of everything read; consequently, the mentee is going to have questions. But the unfortunate fact is: Many mentees don't ask questions, either because they have the preconceived idea that mentors don't like or welcome questions, or they fear that the mentor will chew them out for asking "stupid" questions. So they keep quiet and little learning occurs.

Creating a safe learning environment helps the mentor set the right tone for all interactions with the mentee. By "right," we mean one that is psychologically safe and conducive to learning. A great way to ease the mentee into learning mode is by making references to the pre-observation reading and making it safe for the mentee to ask questions. Invite questions by asking a simple, polite, and noncondescending "Do you have any questions about the reading?" You should respond to those questions in a clear and similarly polite and noncondescending manner. In certain situations, a coaching or nondirective style may be more appropriate than downloading.

Mentor Action 4: Brief the Mentee. With Mentor Actions 2 and 3 put into effect, it's time for Mentor Action 4: Brief the mentee. The pre-observation briefing is particularly important and is aimed at helping your mentee to deepen personal knowledge and understanding of the task and to get the most out of the observation experience. It revolves around two key questions:

- What does the task involve?
- What is the mentee expected to do during observation?

Let's briefly examine each one.

What Does the Task Involve? The mentor should explain the important aspects of the task to the mentee, which include the following six aspects:

- *The reason(s) for performing the task*
  Ask yourself this question: "Why does the mentee need to learn this task and eventually perform it on his or her own?" Your answer will form the basis of your explanation. In addition, the mentor should help the mentee to see clearly the value of the behavior(s) being learned. The mentee must believe that the behaviors learned will help in progress toward his or her overarching goal. If the mentee is not convinced, he or she won't be motivated to learn.

- *The role(s) and responsibilities of the mentee*
  Role and responsibilities are, to a large extent, clear-cut in situations where only you and your mentee are involved in the task. Nevertheless, the mentor should not assume anything and still brief the mentee on this important topic. In situations where the task involves many steps and people other than the mentor and mentee, clarity of role(s) and responsibilities becomes critically important. In a group or team environment, the mentor has to make sure that the mentee knows the "part" or "parts" of the task that the mentee "owns."

- *The tools and resources to perform the task*
  This part of the briefing should be quite straightforward for the mentor. You need to include equipment, data, information, books, websites, and people, as well as how to access them. Additionally, what the mentor could do to add value is to provide practical advice. Practical advice includes tips that will help the mentee to perform the task more efficiently or effectively. Here are some questions to jumpstart your thinking:
  - *Is there a "better" tool or resource to perform the task better?* Some mentors are more effective or efficient than other people because they know how to select the most

appropriate tool or resource for the task in question or they utilize nonstandard ones. If you will recall, Doris intubates newborn babies without using the stylet, which is a nonstandard approach. The reason Doris did so was to minimize the risk of injury to the windpipe.

○ *Are there obstacles to the task?* For example, bottleneck situations or other constraints.

○ *Is there a "right" time (e.g., time of day or year) to perform the task?* For example, some tasks are best done in the morning, whereas some in the wee hours of the night. Here's another example: some tasks are best done during a particular season (e.g., winter, spring, or monsoon).

○ *Is there any advice that isn't tool- or resource-related you can give to help your mentee perform the task better?* For example, appropriate attire or posture. Think along (or even out of) these lines, and we are sure you can come up with lots of good practical advice for your mentee.

- *The boundaries of the task*
  Work is a process. In all likelihood, your mentee will need some sort of input (e.g., data, information, or raw materials) from someone or somewhere before being able to start the task. When the mentee is done, what is done with the mentee's output? In all likelihood, the mentee will hand it over to someone. Your mentee should know all these things.

  The mentor can prepare for this part by asking a set of questions: *Where does the task start? And where does it end? How does the task start? And how does it end?* The mentor may also want to explain how the task in question is connected to everything else. By doing so, the mentor is expanding the mentee's horizons and offering a glimpse of the bigger picture, which can be highly motivating.

- *The performance standards*
  Performance is usually evaluated along two key dimensions: process and outcome. Process is about how the task is done,

whereas outcome is about what the task produces. Typical process indicators include time (e.g., was the deadline met) and cost (e.g., was the task completed within the agreed-upon budget). An indicator that is closely linked to process is behavior. Specifically, we are referring to behaviors that exemplify the values held in high regard by the mentor or the mentee's organization. For example, if teamwork is a value, a relevant question would be "Was the task performed in a manner that reflected good teamwork?" Last but not least are the outcome indicators, which normally include quantity and quality.

Your mentee must have a clear picture of what satisfactory performance looks like. So let your mentee know all the relevant performance standards (as defined by the mentee's organization or mentor) that must be fulfilled. In addition, the mentee needs to know who is going to evaluate mentee performance and when. In the "pre-release" period, that is, Phases 1 and 2, it is typically the mentor who conducts the evaluation. In the "post-release" period, that is, the period after the end of Phase 2, the evaluator could either be the mentor or a third party.

- *The consequences*

Both performance and nonperformance have consequences. Performance could result in the mentee achieving a goal or at least getting one step closer to it. In some cases, an external reward may be waiting for the mentee (e.g., monetary reward, promotion). Consequences of nonperformance are typically punitive in nature (e.g., getting fired or a demotion), but that is not the only kind. Some consequences are physical or psychological in nature. For instance, a mentee who uses a piece of equipment wrongly could end up injured. Or, perhaps worse, the mentee could end up hurting someone else and the psychological pain that follows can be excruciating. The bottom line: Your mentee should be aware of all the key consequences. But don't overemphasize the negative—you don't want to scare the mentee into paralysis!

What Is the Mentee Expected to Do During Observation? The most important thing that the mentee must do is to pay attention to the right things, and the mentor can help in a big way to direct the mentee's attention to them.

For a start, the mentor can instruct the mentee to pay closer attention to the things that he or she found interesting or confusing in the pre-observation reading.

Second, the mentor may want to draw the mentee's attention to a specific step or steps. This attention is especially useful for complex tasks that entail many aspects. Just before you go into action, give your mentee a heads-up: "Watch how I perform this task."

Third, draw the mentee's attention to your distinct way of doing things. By "distinct," we mean the things that you do differently from other people that give you an edge over them; "things" include but are not limited to style, method, or technique. In the Doris-and-Jane story, Doris told Jane about her unconventional yet effective way of intubation and later showed her mentee how to do it. Her method is an example of "distinct."

Finally, ask your mentee to use the appropriate senses (e.g., sight, hearing, smell, taste, and touch) when observing. Some mentees are required to make more intense use of their senses than others. For instance, some of the people who do forensics (think *CSI*, the television series) are expected to use nearly all of their five senses at all times. Those involved in the culinary arts are often expected to do likewise. For the rest of us, it's mainly "sights and sounds." Sights refer to observable behaviors, which we've already discussed extensively, while sounds refer to communication. If communication is a significant factor in task success, the mentee should then be urged to listen attentively to what the mentor says plus when and how the mentor says it.

All the pre-observation Mentor Actions are aimed at helping your mentee to get the most out of the observation experience, so you should make time for them. They won't be too time-consuming because they're not as hard as they seem. Furthermore, if you think expansively, you'd find that you can perform these actions almost any-where. Here are some ideas to get you started:

- Talk in the car or cab, when the two of you are on your way to a meeting
- Talk over breakfast, lunch, or dinner
- Talk at the airport or on the plane, then talk some more in the evenings at the hotel over a drink

As you can see, there are many opportunities to prepare your mentee. Just remember: In order for them to be effective, the preparations must be done before the actual observation.

Phase 1B: Observation

In Phase 1B, the mentor models the execution of a task, and the mentee observes the execution. For this phase, we recommend two Mentor Actions: "Keep it simple and straightforward" and "Educate where possible."

Mentor Action 5: Keep It Simple and Straightforward (KISS). A task is a single activity that can be completed in a series of steps. It is just the right "unit of observation" for the mentee because it is neither too simple nor too complicated. The mentor should note the word *single* in our definition. We stress limiting mentor modeling to one *single* task per (observation) session and refrain from modeling multitasking. The reason for modeling only one is that a mentee who watches two or more tasks at one time is more likely to suffer information or sensory overload and end up confused. (The same mentor may of course model a different task at a different time for the same mentee.)

Mentor Action 6: Educate, Educate, Educate. How the mentor models a task depends on the nature of the task. Some tasks or steps within a task require the mentor's complete concentration. Attention-intensive tasks include those involving the use of firearms and certain medical procedures. During such tasks, little or no communication between the mentor and mentee can or should occur. On the other hand are tasks that pose virtually no threat to life or limb. Cooking and public speaking are examples of such tasks. Hence, at the end of the day, the mentor will have to exercise discretion on whether to speak up or keep quiet.

But wherever possible, the mentor should endeavor to educate. That is, the mentor should think of ways to help the mentee to absorb the observational learning and grab every reasonable opportunity to reinforce that learning. For instance, a mentor can do so by providing a running commentary on what he or she is doing. A mentor can also encourage the mentee to take notes, if it's allowed and practical.

Phase 1C: Post-Observation

Phase 1C, otherwise known as post-observation, is the third and final subphase of Phase 1. This subphase contains only one Mentor Action, namely "Mentor-mentee team reflection."

Mentor Action 7: Mentor-Mentee Team Reflection. Reflecting is a practice not usually associated with modeling. So why is it present in Modeling 2.0? One major reason it's included is because reflection is powerful a learning tool (see previous chapter). Furthermore, it's a great opportunity to introduce the mentee to the skill of reflection. You will see reflection in both Phases 1 and 2.

However, the type of reflection recommended for Mentor Action 7 is different from the one that you read about earlier. Here, the mentor and mentee are to reflect collectively as a mentor-mentee team. In team reflection, the mentor uses reflection to teach and the mentee benefits. Another difference is that the team reflection done in Mentor Action 7 need not be the full-blown reflection as per the previous chapter. Nevertheless, important similarities exist between the two types: Both are powered by questions.

How to team-reflect. After every observation, invite the mentee to sit down and reflect on what was just observed. Remember "safety first"—Mentor Action 3, "create a safe learning environment," is in effect as long as you're mentoring. Encourage the mentee to ask questions with the perennially useful "Do you have any questions about the observation?" And always answer them in a polite and non-condescending way.

The questions that will emerge during the reflection depend on what was observed and on the mentee. Anecdotal evidence suggests that the mentee will mainly be "in fact-finding mode" (as one mentor puts it) in this Phase. That is, the mentee will tend to ask questions in order better understand the observation in particular and the task in general. Hence, the questions in Phase 1 are predominantly the who, what, where, when, which, and how questions. Such questions may seem superficial, but they are nevertheless a good way of getting a learning conversation going. You may occasionally be asked one or two "tough" questions in Phase 1; it doesn't happen too often, but do expect the questions to get tougher as time goes by.

The mentor may use a coaching style when appropriate. For example, you may use this style with mentees who have had the chance to observe the same task more than once. In such situations, you get to ask some questions, but make sure they are questions that will stimulate the mentee's thinking. Why questions are great for intellectual stimulation. For instance, "Why do you think this step was necessary?"

Finally, encourage your mentee to engage in self-directed learning through self-reflection wherever appropriate. Share with the mentee what you know about it and, more important, show him or her how to do it. (If you need a refresher, you can reread the previous chapter.)

Exhibit 7-1 displays a summary of all the Mentor Actions in Phase 1.

Phase 2

An enormous variety of tasks in the real world, not forgetting their variegated nuances of complexity, occupy us humans. Hence, no one-size-fits-all approach can be applied to Phase 2, which is primarily about doing. Nevertheless, a number of practices are common between and among the approaches. We shall focus on and describe these commonalities, discuss the issues usually associated with them, and suggest ways to deal with those issues.

Exhibit 7-1: Mentor Actions in Phase 1

Phase 1A: Pre-Observation

- Mentor Action 1: Create "watching opportunities."
- Mentor Action 2: Assign pre-observation reading.
- Mentor Action 3: Create a safe learning environment.
- Mentor Action 4: Brief the mentee.

Phase 1B: Observation

- Mentor Action 5: Keep it simple and straightforward (KISS).
- Mentor Action 6: Educate, educate, educate.

Phase 1C: Post-Observation

- Mentor Action 7: Mentor-mentee team reflection.

Common Practice 1: Teaching by Example

Every mentor should be aware of opportunities: Whenever your mentee can see you in action, he or she can learn from your actions. It also means that you can and should teach by example in such situations. Because your mentee can still see you in Phase 2, you can continue to teach this way.

In Phase 2, the teaching can be about task competence, interpersonal competence, or both. Since we've already discussed task competence at length in Phase 1, we will discuss interpersonal competence here.

If you will recall, we urged you in Phase 1 (Mentor Action 4) to draw your mentee's attention to the way you communicate if communication is instrumental to the success of the task you're executing. In most cases, it is. Moreover, communication is an integral part of interpersonal competence. And interpersonal competence is critically important because most work gets done in teams or groups or in collaboration with external parties (e.g., suppliers, customers, government). If the working relationships aren't working well, the work suffers. Given its significance, interpersonal competence should be a modeling goal, along with task competence.

The mentee can learn from your interactions with other people. The mentee can also learn from interactions with you. For example, in the Doris-and-Jane story, Jane went straight into action after two observations, albeit under the watchful eye of her mentor. She was nervous about her first intubation, so Doris offered her mentee some words of encouragement to help her regain her composure. After having reflected on that episode, Jane told us that she would adopt that "encourager behavior." Why did Jane find that behavior so compelling? She explained that some senior doctors behave in the same way that Dr. Gregory House does. (Dr. House is the protagonist in the highly popular television series, *House*.) That is, the seniors would "chew people up and spit them out," ridiculing their mentee or subordinate in private or in public. As a result, "people feel miserable, morale is low, and work sometimes feels meaningless." But Doris, through her behavior, taught Jane that *House*-like behavior is unnecessary. Instead, everybody ought to be treated with respect. Doris's words had a positive and uplifting effect on Jane, so Jane was quite certain that similar words would have a similar effect on other people, which is why Jane wants to copy that particular behavior.

As you can see, teaching by example is powerful.

Common Practice 2: Learning by Doing

Doing is a common and powerful form of mentee learning in Phase 2. Learning by doing is a manifestation of an age-old principle whose efficacy is rarely, if ever, in question.

Doing, in this case, *mainly* means copying or imitating the mentor's task-related behaviors. In light of this definition, the implication for the mentor is clear: A mentor must let the mentee do. Delegation is one common way to address this implication.

Teaching Through Delegation. In delegation the mentor shifts some or all task-related decision-making authority to the mentee. The mentor begins the process by first assigning the mentee an entire task or a part thereof (e.g., a single step or several steps of a task). The mentee is then given the responsibility to complete this assignment in a manner that meets the agreed-upon performance standards. To enable the mentee to fulfill his or her responsibility, the mentor should delegate authority that is equal to the responsibility. When delegation has occurred, the mentee gets to make his or her own decisions and act independently. That is, the mentee can decide without consulting with the mentor.

Now every mentor knows about delegation, but knowing about it doesn't mean it is done right all the time. If it isn't done right, it fails. And if it fails, people stop delegating or are fearful of doing it. To be more precise, it is the consequences of failure that people find unnerving. Let's suppose that a mentor delegates part of a task to a mentee, and the two share responsibility for the task outcome; if the task fails (due largely to the mentee's nonperformance), the fallout resulting from the failure may tarnish the mentor's reputation or damage his or her credibility.

Great mentors, however, see the value in delegation and believe it can achieve the following:

1. *It develops mentees and builds confidence.* With delegation, the mentee gets to practice what was learned, which can be a good starting point for mentee development. And the more the mentee practices, the more confident the mentee becomes.
2. *It improves mentor-mentee relationship.* Delegation is one of the best ways for the mentor to show confidence in the mentee. The show of support often leads to a better relationship between the two.

Fully aware of the risk of failure, great mentors also make it a point to delegate properly. Here's how.

Step One: Determine what is to be delegated and to whom. Let's consider the "what" first. If a task is simple—that is, if it doesn't involve too many steps or too many people or if it isn't time-consuming—then delegate the entire task to the mentee. Mentors however should be aware that some simple tasks, when they fail, can have serious repercussions. Remember the intubation procedure in the Doris-and-Jane story? It's actually a simple task with potentially serious consequences. Simple because a doctor must complete it in less than 20 seconds. Serious because when it's done wrong, it can result in windpipe damage. What about a complex task? It has steps, just like all other steps. And the mentor can choose to delegate a single step or several steps to the mentee. Let's now consider the "whom." The key factor here is mentee competence. Delegate step or steps that you know for sure the mentee is good at so as to incur less chance of task failure. A complementary consideration is to delegate step or steps that you are good at so that in the event of a near-failure, you are better able to contain the damage. Note that these considerations are meant only for the initial part of delegation. As time progresses and your mentee's competence increases, you must make the necessary adjustments and allow delegation to escalate as appropriate. That is, the mentee should graduate from step or steps to entire task eventually.

Step Two: Explain the delegation. You should be familiar with the explaining part—you've already done it in Mentor Action 4 in Phase 1. But this time around, you may have to zoom in on a particular step or steps, especially if you are delegating only a part of the task. A word about performance expectations is also appropriate here. Modeling is not cloning. That is, the mentor should never expect the mentee to exhibit task-related behaviors that are indistinguishable from the mentor's. The mentee will have his or her own way—one that is not identical to that of the mentor—of performing a task. If it is effectual, legal, and ethical, it should be acceptable. Ultimately, the mentor has to differentiate between performance requirements and personal preferences. Unless an overriding need to adhere to specific styles, methods, or techniques is present, the mentor should provide an explanation that focuses mainly on the desired end results.

Step Three: Negotiate the delegation. Delegation is something that shouldn't be imposed on the mentee. For one thing, the mentee will want to decide whether he or she has been given enough authority to complete the task or step successfully. The mentee must go through this step because no mentor is going to delegate to a mentee unlimited authority. A mentee who feels not enough authority has been given from the mentor will likely ask for more, and the negotiation begins. At the end of the day, both partners must reach an agreement that a right amount of authority will be shifting, and both have a clear picture of where the boundaries are and agree to respect them.

Another important thing that is up for negotiation is feedback controls. The main purpose of these controls is to monitor the mentee's progress. They also act as an early warning system for the mentor in that they allow the mentee to make small manageable mistakes but alert the mentor to imminent big ones. The control mechanisms include but are not limited to reporting schedules and periodic spot checks. They should also be negotiated and established at the outset. The mentor should remember that delegation without proper feedback controls is tantamount to abdication.

Step Four: Inform those who are affected. We do not work in a vacuum. When people will be affected by your decision to delegate, you need to inform them. The contents of your communication should include the what and the whom mentioned in Step One—plus the amount of authority that is to be shifted.

If you perform the four steps outlined here, you should be in good shape.

Safety Precautions

Let's face it—delegation isn't a mature or complete science and will probably never be. No matter how good you are at reading an individual, you may still get it wrong. The realistic mentor knows that mistakes are part of delegation and therefore expects and accepts them. After all, mistakes can be good learning experiences for the mentee, as long as their costs to the mentee, mentor, or others are within acceptable limits. In the event you feel the costs are unacceptably high, you must be prepared to pull the plug.

Here are some safety precautions that can help the mentor control the costs:

- *Dry runs first.* Let your mentee do things in a safe environment first. Have the mentee go through a dry run of the task or step.
- *Internal before external.* Tasks or steps within your own organization are generally safer than those done outside. In addition, your mentee will likely feel more comfortable trying out new things among insiders and in familiar surroundings. Finally, internal damage, if any, may be easier to repair.
- *New rather than old.* If the task you are modeling involves frequent contact with the outside world and you have to introduce your mentee to outsiders, then it's best that the mentee makes contact with new people (e.g., new customers or suppliers) with no preexisting baggage. Existing contacts may have an axe to grind, and your mentee may find the situation too hot to handle.

Common Practice 3: Teaching Through Feedback

As in the case of delegation, every mentor knows about feedback. And, again, knowing about it doesn't mean it is done right all the time. To do it right, you must first have the right understanding about feedback.

Feedback is information about the mentee's performance (outcome and/or process) and behavior in relation to the twin goals of task and interpersonal competence. The information can later be used to redirect or reinforce. Redirection is about improving the mentee's performance or behavior. In redirection, the mentor first identifies the things that do not contribute to the twin goals and then offers guidance on the most likely ways to achieve them. When feedback is used for redirection, it is commonly referred to as "constructive feedback." Reinforcement, on the other hand, is about identifying beneficial behaviors that do contribute to the twin goals and encouraging the mentee to replicate them. It's also about motivating the mentee to develop those behaviors further. It can improve the mentor-mentee relationship. "Appreciative feedback" is used in reinforcement.

Before feedback can be given, however, a series of actions must first occur. The starting point is the establishment of performance standards, either by the mentor or the organization to which the mentee belongs (e.g., the mentee's employer, the professional body that is offering the accreditation that the mentee desires). The second step is to communicate the performance standards to the mentee; the mentor will have already done so in Mentor Action 4 in Phase 1. Next is the collection of performance data, based on observations by the mentor. A common misconception about this step is the much-touted need for suspended judgment. Some mentors feel guilty because they cannot suspend judgment during observation. We want to tell you that it's OK to judge, and that you can't be a good observer without using judgment. Let's think about it for a moment. Whenever you observe, you are picking out beneficial or unbeneficial behaviors. Determining which behaviors are beneficial and which are not represents an act of judgment, so judgment is necessary. Even though you should not suspend judgment, you should "presume innocence" on the part of the mentee. Most people don't fail on purpose. As our friend and coaching guru, Tom Crane, puts it: "Most of us are doing the very best we know with the ability and awareness we have at that moment." Hence, always give your mentee the benefit of the doubt. The fourth and penultimate step is performance evaluation. Your mentee should know how and when the evaluation will be conducted and by whom. As mentioned earlier, in the "pre-release" period, that is, Phases 1 and 2, it is typically the mentor who conducts the evaluation whereas in the "post-release" period, that is, the period after the end of Phase 2, the evaluator could either be the mentor or a third party. After that is the fifth and final step, the giving of feedback.

The best feedback is always given with the best intentions. It means that the mentor should offer feedback only in the genuine belief that the feedback would benefit the mentee. The main benefits, as we have seen, can be classified as redirection and reinforcement. Other benefits include inspiration and encouragement. All actionable feedback contains descriptions of specific facts or behaviors and impact (or FBI). Here's what we mean:

- Facts—Describe the situation in which the observed behavior occurred (e.g., meeting, presentation).
- Behavior—Describe the specific behavior that you saw and/or heard and that you thought was significant.
- Impact—Describe the impact of your mentee's behavior on you and/or other people (e.g., those present in the situation).

The words *description* and *specific* are also important. *Description* means using nonjudgmental language, whereas specific means avoiding general or vague statements. "At this morning's meeting, I noticed that you raised your voice somewhat at John, and John was visibly affected by it afterward" is an example of FBI feedback.

Where appropriate, you may add a subjective element to your feedback to motivate or encourage. For example, "Before you responded to Jamie's question, you paused and smiled at him—*I thought that was good*. And he seemed to have reacted positively to your answer." This example is categorized as appreciative feedback. (Feedback, as mentioned, can be divided into appreciative feedback and constructive feedback.) You may use the same "format" for appreciative feedback:

- Describe the specific mentee behavior that you wish to highlight ("Before you responded to Jamie's question, you paused and smiled at him").
- Describe the specific impact that that particular behavior has helped to achieve ("And he seemed to have reacted positively to your answer").

- Insert a compliment somewhere in your statement ("I thought that was good").

Providing constructive feedback, on the other hand, can be a challenge. For one thing (which can be a big thing), your mentee may misconstrue it as a personal attack. Hence, you may have to explicitly state your positive intentions before offering such feedback. And you may have to seek his permission also. It might sound something like this: "Jim, I saw something that you did at this morning's meeting that poses a risk to the teamwork that the team currently enjoys. I've got some ideas that might help mitigate that risk. Have you got a few minutes now or would later be better?" Once you get the all-clear from your mentee, you repeat many of the things that you just saw in appreciative feedback. You include the facts and/or behaviors and also the impact. You, of course, omit the compliment. Another key difference is the addition of a moment of silence. That is, after delivering the FBI, you pause to let your mentee process the feedback and respond. Finally, you wrap things up with possibilities, which is another key difference. In "possibilities," you ask your mentee about the ways in which he or she could have behaved more effectively. You may also want to offer your own recommendations.

When you follow the suggestions outlined in Common Practice 3, we are certain that your feedback will be impactful.

What Happens After Phase 2

What happens *after* Phase 2? One thing's for sure—the mentee graduates from the task in question. Another thing's for sure too—the relationship *need not* end. If the mentee has to master another task and the mentor is able to provide the appropriate modeling, the relationship continues. Even when the mentor can't provide what the mentee is looking for, their relationship can still continue. Not as a mentorship, but as a friendship.

The two able and independent individuals can now choose to enter into interdependent, synergistic collaborations. Or they can choose to simply inspire, motivate, or encourage each other. Whatever their choice, "prosper thy neighbor" should be their guiding principle.

CHAPTER 8

THE STORYTELLING MENTOR

"Storytelling is the most powerful way to put ideas into the world today."
—Robert McAfee Brown

Storytelling at the Workplace: A Brief Introduction

Interest in workplace storytelling, both oral and written, has surged over the past 15 years or so. A large number of books and articles are devoted to the subject and targeted at academics and practitioners. The fact that *Reader's Digest* would run a story on storytelling (i.e., Clark, 2007) is a crude but accurate barometer of just how mainstream the practice has become.

We can also gain insight from knowing who is practicing storytelling. Here is a partial list of organizations that are doing so:

- 3M (Shaw, Brown, and Bromiley, 1998)
- Eli Lilly (Harris and Barnes, 2006)
- FedEx (Clark, 2007)
- IBM (Denning, 2004)
- NASA (Anonymous, 2005; Pink, 2006)
- Nordstrom (Collins and Porras, 2002)
- Ritz-Carlton (Maxwell and Dickman, 2007)
- Xerox (Denning, 2004)

These organizations can be categorized in two ways. Under Category 1 are organizations whose association with storytelling probably won't strike a person as a complete surprise. Firms that may be placed under Category 1 include FedEx, the logistics solutions provider; Nordstrom, the North American retailer; and Ritz-Carlton, the international hotel chain.

Organizations under Category 2 are those that may have surprised or even shocked you—you totally did not expect them to practice storytelling at all. Possible candidates include IBM, NASA, and Xerox. Why them? To start with, IBM and Xerox are both large technology companies, whereas NASA (National Aeronautics and Space Administration) is a heavy user of technology. These organizations are filled predominantly with technical people. Technical people are known to be left-brained, analytical people—people who want facts and figures, not stories. So why on earth are these firms using storytelling, something that is so right-brained and seems so touchy-feely?

We can certainly conclude that storytelling is somehow useful, given the interest shown by executives across a wide range of industries. If it were not so, they would not have bothered with it. Not surprisingly, our research reveals that its usefulness extends to mentoring. For example, mentors at the pharmaceutical firm Eli Lilly (Harris and Barnes, 2006) and IBM (Murrell, Forte-Trammell, and Bing, 2009) have used storytelling and are convinced that it benefits their mentoring. We are just as convinced, and we think mentors should take full advantage of the power of storytelling.

Hence, this chapter. Here, you will learn about the effective use of stories in mentoring. When you are done reading, you will know what mentoring stories are like, what makes them powerful, and how to use them powerfully in the *oral* mode.

Mentoring Stories

A mentoring story is a special kind of story. It is a *story* that compels its listener to *think* or *act in a different way*. Let's take several key words or phrases in the preceding definition (all italicized) and examine them one by one.

Story

The mentor should expand his or her thinking about what a story is. In an insightful *Harvard Business Review* article, Stephen Denning, one of the world's foremost experts in organizational storytelling, writes that every kind of story has a place in the workplace, with a time for the "traditional" story (one with, among other things, a plot as well as a hero) and for the nontraditional one (one that doesn't contain many of the traditional elements). Therefore, the mentor need not limit himself or herself to any kind of story, which is actually both good news and bad. The good news is that the mentor has plenty of options. The bad news—a plethora of choices makes story selection tough. Not to worry, though, we know just the kind of story that works for mentors. That, of course, is the "mentoring story," and we'll show you what one looks like.

At the same time, Denning (2008, p. 132) stresses that storytelling is merely a "tool": one that helps the storyteller to achieve his or her "objectives." The two takeaways here for the mentor are (1) the objective is more important than the story and (2) the story must do its intended job.

But what, indeed, can a mentoring story do? As suggested in our definition, mentoring stories produce two possible *broad* outcomes:

- Thinking in a different way
- Acting in a different way

Both outcomes reflect change, and both are important. Let us now consider them individually.

Thinking in a Different Way

Thinking in a different way refers to a change in *what* and/or *how* your mentee thinks. It is an inward change. It is not visible to the naked eye and cannot be easily detected. Even though you cannot see it, it doesn't mean it is not there. Nor is it unimportant. Psychologists tell us that what we think is what we do. That is, our thoughts are the precursors of our actions. And a real, permanent change in thought will almost always result in a change in behavior (or outward change).

Acting in a Different Way

In the context of our discussion, acting in a different way means that your mentee is acting with either increased efficiency or effectiveness. (The change could, of course, be a mix of efficiency and effectiveness.) Efficiency: He or she is doing something faster, better, cheaper, or a combination thereof. Effectiveness: He or she is doing the important things and not just the urgent ones.

Acting in a different way is an outward change, one that other people can readily observe. It can happen soon after the storytelling or further down the road. If it happens sooner rather than later, it does not necessarily mean that the mentoring story has bypassed the thinking step that we talked about earlier. It just means that the mentoring story has accelerated that step. Do not be disappointed if the desired change does not occur immediately. Time delays between thinking and doing do happen. However, if the desired change is taking too long, you might want to try another story.

The Characteristics of Mentoring Stories

We mentioned in the previous section that the mentor can use pretty much any kind of story. We of course recommend the mentoring story. Before we show you what it looks like, let's begin with SEAL.

SEAL stands for **Short, Entertaining, Audience-appropriate**, and **Learning-oriented**. Together, these four characteristics give mentoring stories their power. Let us now consider each characteristic briefly.

Short

The mentoring story is short. In fact, it is essentially an anecdote. Why short? Because in the modern workplace, most people, including your mentee, have neither the time nor the patience for a long story. The brevity also helps you to maintain the listener's attention.

Entertaining

The mentoring story is entertaining. In this context, entertaining refers to the story's ability to grab the mentee's attention and hold on to it. A great mentoring story pulls the mentee away from a world full of distractions and then helps him or her to focus on the story and its key learning point.

Audience-Appropriate

This characteristic is *the* key. Because of its importance, we'll spend more time discussing it. The audience, of course, refers to the mentee. Therefore, what is appropriate to the mentee will be audience-appropriate. But what is appropriate to the mentee?

Two factors determine appropriateness: The mentees themselves and the context. First, what is appropriate is **mentee-dependent**; that is, it is dependent on the listener. This factor is connected to the contents of the story. For example, a typical story contains characters. Can your mentee relate to or identify with the principal characters? If he or she can't, your story, no matter how well told, won't have power.

Second, what is appropriate is also **context-dependent**; it is dependent on the mentee's situation. For example, mentors are aware that their mentees have learning needs. Those needs change over time, however. The storytelling mentor should therefore focus on the mentee's greatest need or needs at a particular point in time.

Discovering what is audience-appropriate requires open and honest communication between the mentor and mentee. For a start, the mentee can help the mentor by highlighting certain needs he or she thinks the mentor can address. But sometimes, partly due to inexperience, mentees may be blind to some of their own needs. So mentors have to use their experience or wisdom to make appropriate suggestions. A mentor should ask himself or herself: What does my mentee need to learn at this particular point in time?

An intimate understanding of the mentee is also helpful. For instance, if your mentee happens to be a sports enthusiast, he or she will probably respond positively to sports stories. Even so, you have to pick the right sport and the right team or star to make your story work. The point here is: Always tell stories that your mentee can relate to.

Learning-Oriented

Every mentoring story must have a learning point, and your job as a storyteller is to help your mentee to at least *understand* it. Many of you may have this question on your minds: What can be learned through mentoring stories? In a nutshell, two things: Knowledge and values. The two correspond to the two broad outcomes—thinking in a different way and acting in a different way—respectively.

- **Knowledge**
  Scholars divide knowledge into explicit knowledge and tacit knowledge.

  Explicit knowledge is knowledge that can be articulated without much difficulty. Things like standard operating procedures and instruction manuals are forms of explicit knowledge. Tacit knowledge, on the other hand, is what people know but rarely articulate. That the articulation does not occur as frequently as it should is partly due to the challenges related to it. For example, the mentor who always seems to know how to get things done in a team environment has tacit knowledge. That knowledge typically contains know-how that cannot be easily captured in words. Furthermore, some of it is so deeply embedded in the mentor (e.g., the mentor's charming personality that disarms fellow team members) that it cannot be separated from him or her. Finally, that knowledge usually goes unnoticed if the mentor remains in the company. However, when the mentor leaves and that valuable knowledge vanishes, people start to sit up and pay attention. But it will be too late by then.

  Therefore, tacit knowledge has to be articulated and stories are an imperfect but nevertheless great way to do so. Storytelling encourages the mentors to reflect on their work and distill learning from their experiences. It is a conscious effort to make explicit the tacit. And where the learning is less transmittable, vivid analogies or metaphors are added into the mix to facilitate transmission.

- **Values**

Values are essentially principles. They can either be personal or organizational. In the context of this chapter, personal values are principles that are important to the mentor, whereas organizational values are principles that are important to the mentee's company. Mentors are, of course, expected to teach their mentees not only personal values but also organizational values.

The desired goal is to produce mentees who can translate values into day-to-day behaviors. The translation process can, however, go wrong. One of the reasons for mistranslation is that values are abstract and therefore subject to misinterpretation. For instance, many of today's organizations say "innovation" is one of their values. But innovation means different things to different organizations. At some organizations, innovation can mean only one thing: An innovation must be new to the world. At others, the adoption of innovations from elsewhere is perfectly acceptable.

In order to prevent misinterpretation, mentors and organizations must somehow find a way to concretize their abstract values. Stories are a solution. They show the listener in a concrete way how a hero or heroine acts out a particular value, and how the listener can emulate the heroic actions. They can also stimulate the listener's imagination and help them come up with ways as to how they might act in their own situations.

One such story is the Art Fry story. Art Fry is the inventor of the wildly successful Post-It notes. And 3M, Art Fry's employer, is telling his story to all its aspiring innovators. Through the telling and retelling of the Art Fry story, 3M hopes to educate its employees on how to innovate (Collins and Porras, 2002).

Heath and Heath (2007) further recommend that great workplace stories should contain only one learning point, no more, no less. If it contains less than one, it's then a pointless story. If it contains more than one, it's simply confusing—as someone once said, "If you say three things, you don't say anything."

The Heaths' recommendation is a good one. Hence, while preparing for your storytelling, you have to first identify *the* key learning point of your story. That is, however, easier said than done—some stories have multiple learning points. Not to worry, here is a simple exercise to help you isolate the one point.

First, have your story ready. Next, set aside some time to ponder the following sentence, then fill in the blanks:

The single, most important thing that I must communicate to my mentee through my story is

_____

_____

_____

_____

_____

_____

_____

_____

_____

Your response to the exercise is the key learning point—the one point you want your mentee to learn. Use the Worksheets appearing in Exhibits 8-1 through 8-6 to identify some important, memorable stories to share with a mentee.

Exhibit 8-1: A Worksheet to Identify Your Most Difficult Story

Directions: Use this worksheet to identify a story of value to a mentee. For each question appearing in the left column, provide an answer in the right column. Then be prepared to share the story with your mentee.

Most Difficult Situation Story *What is the most difficult situation you ever faced in your career and in your job in this organization?*		Your Answers
1	What happened? Describe the story step-by-step.	
2	Who was involved? *(Give job titles but no names.)*	
3	When did this occur?	
4	Why was it so difficult?	
5	What did you do in the situation?	
6	What happened as a result of what you did?	
7	If you faced the same situation again, would you handle it the same way? Why or why not?	

Exhibit 8-2: A Worksheet to Identify a Story About Your Most Common Daily Challenge

Directions: Use this worksheet to identify a story of value to a mentee. For each question appearing in the left column, provide an answer in the right column. Then be prepared to share the story with your mentee.

Most Common Daily Challenge Story *What is the most common challenge you face in your job in this organization? Think of your biggest daily challenge.*	Your Answers
1 What happens? Describe the story step-by-step.	
2 Who is involved? *(Give job titles but no names.)*	
3 When does this occur?	
4 Why is it so challenging?	
5 What do you do in the situation?	
6 What happens as a result of what you do?	
7 What advice do you have about dealing with this daily challenge?	

Exhibit 8-3: A Worksheet to Identify Your Biggest Ethical Challenge

Directions: Use this worksheet to identify a story of value to a mentee. For each question appearing in the left column, provide an answer in the right column. Then be prepared to share the story with your mentee.

Biggest Ethical Challenge Story *What is the biggest ethical challenge you ever faced in your job in this organization?*		Your Answers
1	What happened? Describe the story step-by-step.	
2	Who was involved? *(Give job titles but no names.)*	
3	When did this occur?	
4	Why was it ethically challenging?	
5	What did you do in the situation?	
6	What happened as a result of what you did?	
7	What advice would you give others in addressing a similar ethical challenge?	

Exhibit 8-4: A Worksheet to Address What Motivates You Most

Directions: Use this worksheet to identify a story of value to a mentee. For each question appearing in the left column, provide an answer in the right column. Then be prepared to share the story with your mentee.

Most Motivating Story *What is the most exciting, energizing, and motivating experience you ever faced in your job in this organization?*		Your Answers
1	What happened? Describe the story step-by-step.	
2	Who was involved? *(Give job titles but no names.)*	
3	When did this occur?	
4	Why was it so motivating?	
5	What did you do in the situation?	
6	What happened as a result of what you did?	

Exhibit 8-5: A Worksheet to Address What Motivates You on a Daily Basis

Directions: Use this worksheet to identify a story of value to a mentee. For each question appearing in the left column, provide an answer in the right column. Then be prepared to share the story with your mentee.

Daily Motivational Story *What do you experience on the job in the organization every day that you find most exciting and motivating?*		Your Answers
1	What happens? Describe the story step-by-step.	
2	Who is usually involved? *(Give job titles but no names.)*	
3	When does this occur?	
4	Why is it so motivating?	
5	What do you do in the situation?	
6	What happens as a result of what you do?	

Exhibit 8-6: A Worksheet to Address What You Value Most

Directions: Use this worksheet to identify a story of value to a mentee. For each question appearing in the left column, provide an answer in the right column. Then be prepared to share the story with your mentee.

Value Story *What situation can you describe that emphasizes what you value most about your organization and job?*		Your Answers
1	What happened? Describe the story step-by-step.	
2	Who is usually involved? *(Give job titles but no names.)*	
3	When did this occur?	
4	Why does this story or situation illustrate what you value most about the organization and/or your job?	
5	What did you do in the situation?	
6	What happened as a result of what you did?	

Analysis of a Mentoring Story
(And Some How-Tos)

Now that you've learned the basics, it's time to look at an *actual* mentoring story and analyze it through the lens of SEAL. Here is one told by Ray Kroc, the founder of the highly successful fast-food restaurant chain, McDonald's.

When I was running McDonald's from the Oakbrook, Illinois, headquarters, I often drove by the chain's Chicago-area restaurants and would occasionally stop to check things out. One sunny July afternoon, I pulled into a McDonald's parking space and noticed that the flowering bushes were littered with shake cups, Happy Meal boxes, napkins and other trash. Inside, I asked for the manager. Only the assistant manager was there, so I had him call the manager and waited for the anxious man to rush in after a speedy drive from his nearby home. "What can I do for you sir?" the manager asked me. I led him to the parking lot, pointed at the shrubbery and said, "Look! We don't want trash around our sites!" In a matter of minutes, I, my driver, and the manager had picked all the garbage out of the bushes (Dennehy, 1999, pp. 42–3).

Is It Short?

Yes. The trick is to keep your mentoring story under five minutes.

Is It Entertaining?

Yes, it is. You can use any of several ways to make your mentoring story entertaining. The Ray Kroc story makes use of three. First, it contains details. Here are some examples:

- The "shake cups, Happy Meal boxes, [and] napkins" that make up the "trash"

- The "anxious" restaurant manager's "speedy drive" to meet his big boss

Details contribute to the authenticity of the mentoring story, and authenticity helps to sustain the listener's interest.

Second, it contains emotions. The emotions displayed in this story include:

- Anxiety, experienced by the restaurant manager.
- Displeasure. Ray Kroc was obviously upset. Although it is not explicitly stated that Kroc felt so, the listener can easily determine his emotional state through the words or the performance of the story.

Like details, emotions help to keep the story authentic and entertaining.

Third, it contains surprise. Surprise is often found in the unexpected or incongruous.

- One surprise in the Ray Kroc story is this: The restaurant manager clearly did something wrong, but he wasn't punished for it. Ray Kroc was instead more interested in fixing the problem than in meting out punishment.
- Another surprise: Ray Kroc led by example—he led the cleanup. Remember his position and status: He was the big boss, the number one man. He could have just given instructions and then watched from the sidelines. But he didn't.

Note that learning points are usually found in the surprising part of the story.

ANOTHER WAY TO CREATE SURPRISE

One common way to create surprise is to tell a what-I-learned-from-my-mistake story.

Begin your story with a "self-deprecating opener." Here are some examples:

- "Let me tell you about a time when I really screwed up . . ."
- "Let me tell you a story about something I learned the hard way . . ."
- "I'm going to tell you a story and then ask what you would have done in my place to create a better outcome—because almost anything would have worked better than what I did . . ." (Harris and Barnes, 2006)

Imagine for a moment you're the mentee. What would your response be when you hear the opener? Surprise is the normal reaction. Here is your mentor—someone you admire—admitting that he or she screwed up at some point in the past. Immediately, the mentee sits up, pays attention, and wants to hear more.

The subject matter itself is entertaining. Making a mistake or failing is interesting because the mentor standing before the mentee today is obviously *not* a failure. So how did the mentor pull off the turnaround? The mentee will certainly want to find out. (To be sure, success stories work, too. But stories about failures can just be as interesting, if not more. So mentors shouldn't avoid failure stories.)

The self-deprecating opener and the error story also do two things for the mentor: It makes the mentor both humble and human. This is important. The mentor's humility and humanity make it much easier for the mentee to connect with the mentor. And when the connection is there, the attention will be there also.

THE FOURTH WAY

We have so far talked about using details, emotions, and surprise to entertain. The fourth way is called conflict. Conflict comes largely in two flavors:

- The goals or values of one character versus those of another
- The internal conflict—the hero or heroine happens to hold conflicting goals or values at the same time

Here is a conflict-of-values story involving Costco, a U.S. company that operates membership warehouse stores. Its mission is "to continually provide [its] members with quality goods and services at the lowest possible prices." One of its business policies supportive of the mission is the 14 percent maximum markup. In the ensuing story the markup policy becomes a subject of debate and James Sinegal, the company's chief executive officer, is the storyteller.

We were selling Calvin Klein jeans for $29.99, and we were selling every pair we could get our hands on. One competitor matched our price, but they had only four or five pairs in each store, and we had 500 or 600 pairs on the shelf.

We all of a sudden got our hands on several million pairs of Calvin Klein jeans and we bought them at a very good price. It meant that, within the constraints of our markup, which is limited to 14 percent on any item, we had to sell them for $22.99. That was $7 lower than we had been selling every single pair for.

Of course, we concluded that we could have sold all of them (about 4 million pairs) for that higher price almost as quickly as we sold them at $22.99, but there was no question that we would mark them at $22.99 because that's our philosophy.

The conflict in the story can be framed as a question: To make a quick profit (around $28 million in additional profits, to be exact) or to stay true to its mission? The temptation to make more money was no doubt great. But succumbing to it would not have helped Costco "keep faith with the customer." So James Sinegal and his team made the decision to price the jeans at $22.99 (Denning, 2006, p. 46).

Is It Audience-Appropriate?

Appropriateness is affected by both mentee and context. The Ray Kroc story is appropriate if the mentee is a Ray Kroc admirer—that is, he or she knows who Ray Kroc was and admires his achievements or style of management. Such a mentee is more likely to be a McDonald's employee. But that is not always the case—some mentees outside of McDonald's are familiar with Kroc and the Ray Kroc story will work on them too.

The Ray Kroc story is also appropriate if the learning fits the circumstances currently surrounding the mentee. For example, if the mentee is often leading from the sidelines and the mentor thinks that is inappropriate leadership behavior, then the Ray Kroc story is appropriate.

Is It Learning-Oriented?

As we showed earlier in our analysis the Ray Kroc story contains several learning points (see the discussion on the element of surprise). The presence of multiple learning points—a common feature among stories—can be a problem. One potential consequence: What the mentee learns from the story may be different from what you actually want him or her to learn. In this situation, you can do several things. First, you have to decide what you really want to teach through your story. This analysis, in turn, determines its key learning point. Next, you are faced with two alternatives: You could either make it clear what it is that you want your mentee to learn. Or you could check with your mentee on *what* he or she in fact learned.

The former is quite straightforward. The mentor could end the Ray Kroc story by saying:

*The most important thing I want you to learn from the
Ray Kroc story is*

_____

(the key learning point).

The former is, of course, downloading. If you are looking for a less directive approach, go for the latter. This approach will involve questioning. You should avoid overly general questions like "What did you learn from the Ray Kroc story?" Such questions can invite some unexpected, tough-to-handle responses. Instead, use nonthreatening questions to gently guide the mentee:

- What can we learn from Ray Kroc's actions?
- What do you think the restaurant manager learned from this incident?

This way, you can tease the learning out of the mentee. The mentee may provide you with an answer different from the one you're looking for. If that happens, you may prompt further by saying "That's a good answer. What else can we learn from the story?" Then, prompt again if necessary. When the mentee finally produces the desired answer, point it out as the key learning point of the story.

Performing Stories: Some Practical Tips

The final aspect of storytelling is performance. Before you perform, you must prepare. Specifically, you must have stories, stories, and more stories. If you don't have stories, you have nothing to tell. Collecting stories and selecting stories are essential activities in the preparations of a storyteller.

Collecting Stories

You can collect stories from multiple sources. You can collect them from your own experiences, from your friends inside or outside of your organization, or from the media. It doesn't really matter where they come from—as long as they meet two criteria. First, they must be real. You want to stick to nonfiction. As mentioned earlier, real, authentic stories are more entertaining in mentoring. Second, and more important, the story has got to touch you. The more deeply it touches, the more powerful it is. If it doesn't do that, you can't perform it with power later on.

Selecting Stories

Before your mentoring session, go through your story collection and pick out one that is appropriate. As you do so, bear in mind two things: Your audience and the outcome you want to achieve. Use the SEAL criteria to help you select the story and fine-tune it if necessary. Then learn the selected story thoroughly.

Performance

You can improve your storytelling performance by doing two things: Learning by observing and learning by doing.

Learning by Observing

- Observe a professional storyteller in action.
- Observe a workplace storyteller whose storytelling skills you admire in action.
- While observing, pay special attention to the following:
  - How the storyteller creates the mood of the story
  - How the storyteller uses his or her voice (e.g., impersonations)
  - How the storyteller uses eye contact, facial expressions, or gestures
  - How the storyteller paces the story (through pauses, etc.)
  - How the storyteller uses props, if available
- At the end of your observation, discuss your observations with the storyteller.

Learning by Doing

There is no substitute for learning by doing. The more you do it, the better you get. If you are relatively new to storytelling, do it first in a safe environment. Begin by telling a family member your story. Apply what you learned from your observations. Watch your audience for their feedback messages. And don't forget to verbally ask them for feedback. When your confidence level has increased, you should move up by telling stories to your close friends or trusted colleagues. Learn from these experiences. Finally, widen your storytelling circle to include your mentees.

CHAPTER 9

THE PROPER ENDING

"All good things come to an end."
—Anonymous

The End

Since we're nearing the end of this book, we thought it appropriate to talk about "the end." "The end" here refers to the end of a mentoring relationship.

Yes, mentorships do end, as do all other good things. In fact, we shouldn't be surprised that they do. They are meant to be temporary in the first place. The goal is mentee growth and the consequence of that goal is independence. And independence implies some sort of separation.

When the mentee's growth goal has been achieved or changed, it's probably time for you to move on. When you can no longer contribute constructively to the mentee's growth, it's *definitely* time to move on. Moving on does not necessarily mean that you have to end your relationship with your former mentee. It does, however, mean that you have to redefine your relationship with him or her. What will this new relationship look like? A proper ending will help you answer this question.

An improper ending, on the other hand, can have negative consequences. You could, for example, carry the past with you and find it tough to move on. Hauling around that psychological baggage is energy-sapping and soul-withering. All that can be avoided through proper ending.

Mentors should also note that mentorships do not end automatically. They have to be brought to an end. It involves action, and it involves both you and your mentee. So Chapter 9 is about this rarely discussed but important subject. Here, you will learn all the key actions that will help you and your mentee experience a satisfying sense of finality.

How to End Properly

To increase the chances of ending well, a mentor can do several things. They can be categorized under two headings: "Things to do in the beginning and throughout" and "Things to do at the end." These activities are to be understood in the chronological sense. Let us first consider the former.

Things to Do in the Beginning and Throughout

Establish a Clear End Date. Because a temporary thing by definition must end, you should plan for its ending. One practical thing to do is to fix an end date for the mentorship. You should do so at the early stages of your mentoring relationship. But rather than do it unilaterally, discuss it with your mentee to reach a mutual agreement. In formal mentoring, the end date is usually fixed for you by a third party. If it isn't, you can fix it together.

Having an end date also helps the two of you to focus. With an end date in place, you are more likely to pay attention to the things that are goal-relevant and ignore those that are goal-irrelevant.

Talk About the End. Be constantly mindful of the temporariness of the mentorship and the inevitability of completion. Impress those facts upon your mentee and remind him or her as appropriate. These actions are meant to prevent the two of you from becoming overly attached to each other, so that when the time comes for conclusion, it may be easier to detach.

Things to Do at the End

Ending a mentoring relationship is a process and not a one-time act, which means it will stretch over several sessions. The following four elements are important during this period:

Appreciation. Appreciation is about ending things on a high note. It's best to end this way because you would want to transition into the new nonmentoring relationship positively. You may seize the initiative by thanking your mentee for giving you the opportunity and privilege to mentor him or her. You may also appreciate your mentee's strengths, talents or gifts. Say something like: "I admire you for your . . ." and then describe a specific and concrete incident to back it up.

At the same time, allow your mentee to return you the compliments. Everyone could do with a bit of "that" now and then.

Reflection. Reflection here refers to mentor-mentee team reflection. It's about reviewing the mentorship and harvesting the learning. The main purpose of reviewing is to determine whether the goal of the mentorship has been reached. For the review, you may recycle the following Level 1 questions:

- What did we set out to accomplish?
- What did we actually accomplish?

If you did not reach the goal, don't beat yourselves up. Learn from it instead. Ask the question: What could we have done differently to change the outcome?

To harvest the learning, ask the following questions:

- What did you learn? What are the key takeaways?
- What are the implications of that learning?

To encourage the incorporation of that learning into the mentee's work, try this:

- How can you integrate that learning into your work?

You may harvest personal learning also:

- What worked well in our mentorship?
- What do you think I should repeat when I mentor a different person?
- What did you learn about me?

Transition Discussion. This discussion is important. It's about what's next for the both of you. Here, openness and candor are essential. The following questions are helpful:

- What's next for you?
- How should our relationship continue after the mentorship?

At this juncture, you may wish to play a transient, mentor-like role and ask this question: What other developmental opportunities might be helpful for you? If you can connect your former mentee to his or her future mentor, he or she will be grateful to you.

Finally, you should encourage your former mentee to mentor. The world needs them.

Celebration. Celebrations can function as markers—they mark the end of something old and the beginning of something new. So it's good to celebrate at the end of a mentorship. Here are some celebration ideas:

- Give your mentee a gift. Books are good.
- Go out and have a meal together.
- Send an e-mail of congratulation
- Throw a surprise party
- Go wild and actually throw confetti, glitter, or something else associated with celebrations, such as "ticker tape" or ribbons
- Prepare a large banner

- Provide a cake and ice cream, which is associated with birthday parties

The Future: E-Mentoring at Rockwell Collins

Rockwell Collins, a leading aerospace and defense company, launched an online mentoring program that is open to approximately 16,000 employees worldwide. The program is on the cutting edge of mentoring practice, given its use of so-called e-mentoring. Participants, when surveyed about the value of the program, pointed to its benefit in engaging them in company efforts and in transferring knowledge.

Source: Adapted from M. Francis, "Shifting the Shape of Mentoring," *T + D* (September 2009): 36.

CHAPTER 10

BUILDING A MENTORING PROGRAM AND MENTORING CULTURE IN AN ORGANIZATION

"Culture does not change because we desire to change it. Culture changes when the organization is transformed; the culture reflects the realities of people working together every day."
— Frances Hesselbein, "The Key to Cultural Transformation," *Leader to Leader* (Spring 1999)

Mentoring is often a one-on-one effort. Much good mentoring is informal, initiated by someone who desires to learn from someone else believed to be more knowledgeable or more skilled at doing something. But mentoring can also be organized. Indeed, many organizational leaders wish to build the competencies of future leaders (or else transfer the knowledge gained from experience of knowledge workers) through mentoring programs. Executing this kind of transformation requires an organized, systematic effort to guide mentoring, which is different from self-initiated mentoring efforts.

What step-by-step model can help to guide the implementation of a planned mentoring program in an organization? How can mentoring become part of an organizational culture? What challenges must be addressed in building a planned mentoring program in an organization? This chapter addresses these questions.

A Step-by-Step Model to Guide Mentoring Program Implementation

Every good effort has a plan to guide it. Culture change does not happen on its own. It must be planned, implemented, and followed up. Rely on the following model, depicted on the diagram appearing in Exhibit 10-1, to help guide the implementation of a planned mentoring program in an organization.

Step 1: Clarify the Measurable Business Reasons for the Effort and Create Measurable Goals for the Mentoring Program

Most organizational change efforts fail. One reason they do is that their business reasons are not clarified. Even though it might be popular to implement a mentoring program, popularity is not enough. Good business reasons are necessary to support the time, money, and effort required to plan and implement a mentoring program. "It is nice to do" is not a sufficient, compelling reason.

So what might be examples of measurable business reasons to support a mentoring program? Here is a representative (though not comprehensive) list of possible business reasons:

- The organization needs to groom people for greater responsibility to take the place of retiring executives, managers, or supervisors.
- The organization needs to develop people to keep pace with rapid growth.
- The organization needs to build bench strength to engage and retain top performers.

Exhibit 10-1: A Model to Guide Implementation of an Organizational Mentoring Program

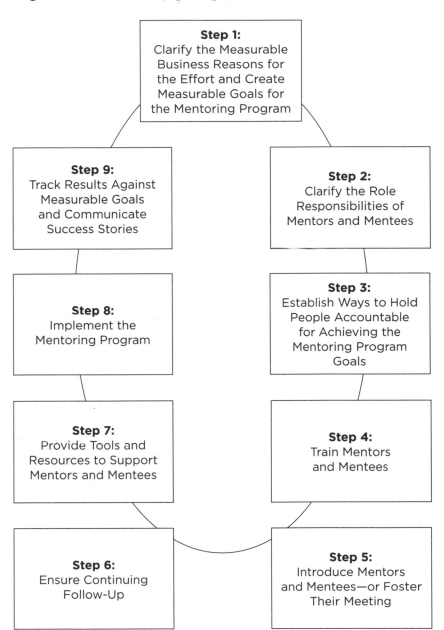

Step 1:
Clarify the Measurable Business Reasons for the Effort and Create Measurable Goals for the Mentoring Program

Step 9:
Track Results Against Measurable Goals and Communicate Success Stories

Step 2:
Clarify the Role Responsibilities of Mentors and Mentees

Step 8:
Implement the Mentoring Program

Step 3:
Establish Ways to Hold People Accountable for Achieving the Mentoring Program Goals

Step 7:
Provide Tools and Resources to Support Mentors and Mentees

Step 4:
Train Mentors and Mentees

Step 6:
Ensure Continuing Follow-Up

Step 5:
Introduce Mentors and Mentees—or Foster Their Meeting

- The organization needs to transfer the knowledge gained from experience by seasoned knowledge workers, such as engineers or IT professionals, to less seasoned workers.

These reasons are made measurable when the need is quantified by setting goals and using additional language that addresses the issue of how these goals are measured.

Step 2: Clarify the Role Responsibilities of Mentors and Mentees

Mentoring programs sometimes fail because people are not clear what they are supposed to do. So spell it out in a "role description."

A piece of advice here: HR professionals should not compile role descriptions on their own. Instead, they should facilitate a task force of managers and workers to write these role descriptions. The responsibilities of a given role are more likely to be "owned" if line (operating) managers have a say in what is in the role descriptions. HR cannot do all the work, and should not be expected to. What is the manager's role as mentor? What is the mentee's role? Write it out. With the writing comes greater understanding and engagement.

Step 3: Establish Ways to Hold People Accountable for Achieving the Mentoring Program Goals

People do not do things just for fun. They have to have a reason. Nor will they perform unless they believe they have some reason to do so. Without accountability, a mentoring program—like just about any other effort—will fail.

Many kinds of accountability systems can be used in this situation. Mentoring, for instance, could be rewarded financially. It could be the focus of an award-and-recognition program. Mentoring could be part of the key performance indicators for managers. Alternatively, mentoring effort could be a factor considered when making promotion decisions.

Lack of willingness could likewise be a focus of punishment, though arm-twisting is rarely an effective strategy. After all, some people are just not cut out to be mentors, and they should not be punished for not being able to do what they do not believe they should do. Still, punishment is an accountability system.

Your organization and its leaders will have to give thought to how to hold people accountable for mentoring. Whichever of the many approaches is used, it should be one that is greeted as fair and equitable by all concerned.

Step 4: Train Mentors and Mentees

Once the business reasons and roles are clear, then people should be trained to be mentors and/or mentees. (Yes, it is possible for one person to be both a mentor to others and a mentee to others.) Such training should be voluntary and open to all interested. Mandatory training is likely to cause more problems than it's worth.

Use the role description for a mentor and build a training outline to show how that role description is carried out. Build in ample opportunities for video-based examples of what to do and what not to do as a mentor. Use role play activities to practice the skills you teach.

The same basic approach should be used when training mentees. The most important difference is that mentees should be clear that they have permission to approach people to be mentors. Their self-confidence should be assessed to determine likely problems they will face due to reluctance to approach higher-status managers or others who may be most useful mentors. Be sure to surface and address frequently asked questions about what mentors should do and what mentees should take responsibility for doing.

Step 5: Introduce Mentors and Mentees— or Foster Their Meeting

One role that the HR department can play in a mentoring program is to find ways to introduce mentors and mentees while also fostering a willingness among mentees to take initiative to seek out their own mentors. Many different approaches can be used in carrying out this step. One way is to identify, during regular talent review meetings, the competencies that individuals need to build to better align their competencies to those required for promotion. Then, for each competency they need to develop, identify one or several people who excel in that competency area and introduce them.

Another way is to solicit a list of people who are willing to be mentors and then circulate that list among those who signal a willingness to be mentees. Encourage one meeting to see how well they get along. Such a meeting can happen over lunch or dinner, perhaps at the organization's expense.

Introductions do not need to be limited to face-to-face interaction. Virtual approaches may also be used, such as e-mail, Skype, Twitter, or similar methods. Mentees can take the lead by approaching those they believe can help them. Then mentees send a current resume and a list of questions to a potential mentor via e-mail.

Yet another way is a variation of so-called speed dating. Possible mentors and mentees can be assigned to each other for a short time, such as 5 minutes, during an event organized for that purpose. The goal is to see how well they are matched interpersonally. Both prospective mentors and mentees can identify individuals they found intriguing, and HR can then match them up for a more in-depth personal meeting.

Step 6: Ensure Continuing Follow-Up

Many worthy programs fail for lack of sustained follow-up. The same is as true of mentoring programs as anything else. Somebody must mind the store, periodically checking "how things are going" with mentors and mentees. Perhaps something as simple as regular e-mails just to ask "How is it progressing?" can signal a willingness to troubleshoot problems that come up or issues that may surface. This role is usually played by HR professionals.

Step 7: Provide Tools and Resources to Support Mentors and Mentees

Tools and resources can be immensely helpful in supporting continuing mentoring relationships. HR professionals can take the lead in providing such tools and resources. Some examples of tools they could supply include the following:

- An agenda to guide an initial meeting between a mentor and a mentee
- A list of questions for a mentor to pose to a mentee
- A list of questions for a mentee to pose to a mentor

Some of these tools can be developed during the training sessions conducted with prospective mentors and mentees, thus ensuring greater buy-in from managers and workers while easing the burden on HR staff. These tools can then be made available online.

Resources to support mentors and mentees might include:

- Online clearinghouses of tools to support mentors and mentees
- Online meeting sites where mentors and mentees who live at a distance can get together
- Online testimonials from the organization's mentors and mentees about the personal and organizational benefits they realized from participating in the mentoring program

Step 8: Implement the Mentoring Program

The preceding steps lead up to this one. Implementation will mean continuing support to ensure that the mentoring program is working and interventions when problems surface. HR professionals sometimes take responsibility for this continuing process of facilitating the program. A high-level steering committee can be appointed to oversee implementation, select individuals to mentor or be mentored, and support continuing program enhancements.

Step 9: Track Results Against Measurable Goals and Communicate Success Stories

A final step is to track results against the measurable goals for the program. The important issue here is to collect information about the business impact of the program. How well did it achieve its intended results as previously identified by decision makers? Of course, additional data can be collected by sending evaluation forms to mentors and mentees, surveying them about how well the program is meeting individual and organizational goals.

As part of evaluation, it is also worthwhile to take time to collect success stories of how the mentoring program has helped both the organization and individuals to achieve their goals. These stories can then be posted on program websites and distributed during training sessions to demonstrate the value of the program, as well as "lessons learned" in the program.

Establishing and Sustaining a Mentoring Culture

A mentoring culture is not established overnight. Magic wands and finger snapping will not make it happen. It takes leaders who are willing to set positive examples, reward others for behavior aligned with the mentoring effort, and devote the necessary time, money, and effort to realize program benefits.

How can you tell if the organization has succeeded in establishing and sustaining a mentoring culture? One way is to ask about it during employee attitude surveys and exit interviews. Another way is to interview successful people in the organization about their perspectives on how much mentoring has helped them succeed. When people regularly cite mentoring by others as an element in their success, then you will know that you have successfully established a mentoring culture.

Identifying and Overcoming Challenges to an Organizational Mentoring Program

Mentoring programs, like many other organizational efforts, will typically face many challenges. Recognize them and be prepared to address them. Among these challenges are:

- The program is not clearly linked to organizational needs.
- The organization's leaders are not clear about why the organization needs a mentoring program.
- The organization's leaders do not agree among themselves on mentoring program goals.
- The mentoring program is not focused around measurable goals.
- The roles of various groups in the effort are not clear.
- No accountability for the program has been established.

Use the tool that appears in Exhibit 10-2 on the following page to involve your organization's decision makers in developing strategies to surmount these typical challenges.

Recognizing that these challenges are common ones is a first step to overcoming them. Beyond that, make sure to show how the mentoring program aligns to organizational needs, establish measurable program goals, secure decision makers' agreement on priorities, measure the effort, and be sure accountabilities of some kind exist.

Concluding Thoughts

This final chapter has described how to move mentoring beyond singular efforts between individuals to an organizational effort. As the chapter indicated, some kind of a model or plan is necessary to guide the process of establishing and implementing the program. Only time and dedicated effort will lead to the change required in establishing a mentoring culture. Common challenges are to be expected when implementing mentoring in organizational settings. A few were listed in the chapter.

The challenge is ultimately yours to ensure that mentoring is successful. Enjoy the challenge!

Exhibit 10-2: A Tool to Overcome Challenges in Implementing a Mentoring Program

Directions: Use this tool to help you identify obstacles to implementing a mentoring program and reach agreement on strategies to overcome those obstacles. For each item in the left column, write ideas in the right column about what might be done to overcome the obstacle. Involve decision makers in this process.

Challenges/Obstacles		Your Answers
1	The program is not clearly linked to organizational needs.	
2	The organization's leaders are not clear about why the organization needs a mentoring program.	
3	The organization's leaders do not agree among themselves on mentoring program goals.	
4	The mentoring program is not focused around measurable goals.	
5	The roles of various groups in the effort are not clear.	
6	No accountability for the program has been established.	

FREQUENTLY ASKED QUESTIONS (FAQS) ABOUT MENTORING

Whenever the issue of mentoring is first discussed, managers and HR professionals typically have many questions. Even though nothing takes the place of in-depth training, this handout is intended to answer some of the most frequently asked questions about mentoring.

Questions and Answers

1. **What is a mentor?**
   A mentor is a role model, teacher, or advisor.

2. **What is the difference between a mentor and a coach?**
   A mentor offers directive advice, telling the mentee what to do; a coach offers less directive suggestions, often using questioning to get individuals to think things out on their own.

3. **Are all mentors the same, or are there different kinds of mentors?**
   There can be different kinds of mentors. A mentor's role has to do with what he or she is good at. If a mentor is good at technical details or solving technical problems, then the mentor can offer help to a mentee on technical issues. If a mentor is good at interpersonal relationships or organizational politics, he or she can offer help to a mentee on those issues. If a mentor is good at

running meetings or at preparing a budget, then the mentor can offer help on those issues.

4. **What should mentors do?**
   The mentor's role is that of helper or advisor. The mentee should usually take initiative in the mentor-mentee relationship, though a mentor can offer advice on what to discuss or what to focus on.

5. **What training is needed to be a mentor?**
   A mentor needs training on the various mentoring techniques and how to function within a relationship that flows from the establishing phase to the enabling and uplifting phase and the exiting phase.

6. **What are the essential qualifications of a mentor?**
   A mentor should be willing to serve as a mentor and should be particularly good at what he or she offers mentoring on.

7. **What should mentees do?**
   Mentees should take responsibility for initiating the mentoring relationship. He or she can ask questions: Posing questions is important. So is a willingness to take initiative in the relationship rather than expecting the mentor to do so. The mentor does not stand to gain as much in the relationship as the mentee and for that reason has little reason to set up and run the meetings. Those efforts should be up to the mentee.

8. **What are the essential qualifications of a mentee?**
   A mentee should be willing to listen, learn, and ask questions. He or she should be willing to take initiative to approach people who can help.

9. **What training is needed to be a mentee?**
   Training for a mentee on how to approach a prospective mentor can be useful, so can training on how to ask questions, how to run meetings, and how to listen for feelings as well as facts.

10. **How do generational differences play a part in mentoring?**
    Take care about jumping to conclusions based on generational

differences. Mentors who assume that all Gen Xers are the same are in for a rude awakening. They are not. It is best for a mentor to ask questions about what the mentee values most and why. Finding out about an individual's background—that is, getting to know him or her—is better than stereotyping people based on their age or sex.

11. **Can a supervisor or manager be a mentor?**
We do not believe so, though not everyone agrees. It seems to us that a supervisor can be a coach. But mentors should usually not have a selfish interest in an individual's development. Direct supervisors do have selfish interests in the future of those reporting to them. A manager or supervisor can be a mentor for those outside their immediate reporting chain but usually not for those who directly report to them.

12. **How can cross-cultural issues affect mentoring?**
Cross-cultural issues *can* affect mentoring. For that reason, it may be useful for a mentee who plans to have a mentor from another culture to also seek out a cultural informant. An *informant* is someone who is from the same culture as the mentor or mentee but is also more familiar with the other culture. The informant can provide insight into issues that are difficult to discuss or cultural issues that may affect the mentor-mentee relationship. Informants can sometimes offer advice on how to bridge cultural differences. It can be wise to cultivate multiple informants because their collective wisdom may be greater than the insights of one person.

13. **How can gender affect mentoring?**
Gender differences can affect mentoring in several ways. First, mentoring across genders (a male mentor and female mentee, or vice versa) can lead to challenges in how others regard the relationship. It can be tough for them to meet for discussions over dinner or lunch because others may gossip. At the same time, it is more advisable to have public meetings than closed-door discussions, which might inspire even more rumors. Second, different

sexes can communicate differently. Training on cross-gender communication can be helpful for mentors or mentees who wish to have a mentor or mentee of the opposite sex.

14. **When do individuals need a mentor?**
Individuals need a mentor when they need help on something—anything.

15. **Who should be a mentor, and who should not be?**
Not everyone is cut out to be a mentor. Some people are philosophically opposed to helping others. To force them to do so is counterproductive. Willingness is the first requirement for an effective mentoring leader.

16. **Who should be a mentee, and who should not be?**
A mentee must be open to asking for, and receiving, help—and listening to others. People who are not open to seeking help or taking advantage of the learning it affords will not be successful as mentees.

17. **How should organizations manage mentoring?**
Many books and articles have been written on how organizations can manage mentoring. Two approaches are common. One is a so-called formal mentoring program in which an organizational group (usually HR) matches two people. Sometimes the organization pays the bill for a first meeting over lunch or dinner. If the relationship continues, the individuals pay for their own future meetings. If the relationship does not continue, then HR tries to find a better match. A second is a so-called informal mentoring program. In that option, HR provides training to prospective mentors and to prospective mentees. But from there on, it is up to would-be mentees to take initiative.

18. **What organizational benefits can result from a mentoring program?**
Mentoring can be an effective way to groom people informally. It can also be useful in transferring knowledge from those who have gained it from experience to those who are less experienced.

Mentoring can thus be an important component of a succession planning or talent management effort.

19. **Why should people be mentors? Mentees?**
When some people reach a certain stage in their lives, they may have a feeling that they should leave a positive legacy. Mentoring can meet a deep need to "leave a legacy." Mentees stand to gain by getting the benefit of others' knowledge and experience.

20. **What's the difference between a mentor and a sponsor?**
A mentor is an advisor; a sponsor opens doors and helps those they help to gain visibility or social contacts that they would not otherwise have available to them.

21. **Is it possible to do virtual mentoring?**
Yes, in fact, it is a very topical subject. Many organizations are experimenting with mentoring done by instant messaging technology, through social media such as Twitter and other programs like Skype or FaceTime.

22. **How does mentoring relate to talent management or succession planning?**
Talent management is about attracting, developing, and retaining the best people; succession planning is about directing attention to the systematic development of people for higher-level responsibility. Mentoring is a way by which to help individuals, or talent pools of people, develop their potential to assume higher-level responsibility. It can also be useful in passing on knowledge gained from experience to those with less experience.

WHAT MENTEES SHOULD DO

This document may facilitate setting expectations. Mentors should modify this document to meet their own expectations for a given mentoring relationship and then hand this (or e-mail it) to the mentee at the beginning of their relationship.

Mentees should:

- Seek out mentors who can help them.
- Assume that they may need more than one mentor to meet all their needs.
- Be clear what their goals are for the mentoring relationship— that is, what they want out of the mentor.
- Take steps to seek out the mentor, communicating on a regular basis as the mentor's schedule permits.
- Prepare for meetings by having an agenda, a list of questions, and documents for review.
- Be civil and respectful of a mentor and his or her time at all times.
- Schedule meetings at times and places of mutual convenience.
- Clarify the basis on which mentor and mentee will communicate— that is, on the job, off the job, by e-mail, through social media, and so forth.

- Expect that they will not always be "told what to do" but asked to "think it out on their own" based on answers to questions they ask.
- Listen carefully to what the mentor says.
- Take notes as appropriate.
- Ask if and when follow-ups can be given (such as revised documents to be reviewed).

COMPETENCIES OF MENTORS AND MENTEES

The Core Competencies of a Mentor

- Credibility
- Ability to establish interpersonal rapport with others and maintain it
- Willingness to mentor
- Questioning skills
- Active listening skills
- Ability to inspire trust
- Self-confidence and self-efficacy
- Politically savvy
- Ability to give clear advice
- Ability to tell compelling, memorable stories that illustrate key concepts
- Ability to show positive regard for others
- Sense of humor
- Ability to control personal biases that may interfere with the mentoring relationship
- Sets a positive example in word and deed

The Core Competencies of a Mentee

- Ability to establish and maintain interpersonal rapport with others
- Willingness to be mentored
- Willingness to take advice
- Questioning skills
- Active listening skills
- Self-confidence and self-efficacy
- Note-taking and memory skills
- Sense of humor

RATING INSTRUMENT FOR MENTORS

Directions: Use this tool to rate yourself on the competencies essential for mentoring. For each competency listed in the left column, rate yourself in the right column. Use this scale: **0 = Not appropriate; 1 = Needs improvement; 2 = Able to demonstrate competency; 3 = Able to demonstrate the competency adequately; 4 = Able to demonstrate the competency very well.** When you are finished, use this tool to plan professional development to improve your mentoring competence.

Mentor Competencies		Ratings				
1	Credibility	0	1	2	3	4
2	Ability to establish interpersonal rapport with others and maintain it	0	1	2	3	4
3	Willingness to mentor	0	1	2	3	4
4	Questioning skills	0	1	2	3	4
5	Active listening skills	0	1	2	3	4
6	Ability to inspire trust	0	1	2	3	4
7	Self-confidence and self-efficacy	0	1	2	3	4
8	Politically savvy	0	1	2	3	4
9	Ability to give clear advice	0	1	2	3	4
10	Ability to tell compelling, memorable stories that illustrate key concepts	0	1	2	3	4
11	Ability to show positive regard for others	0	1	2	3	4
12	Sense of humor	0	1	2	3	4

(continued)

Mentor Competencies	Ratings				
13	Ability to control personal biases that may interfere with the mentoring relationship	O	1	2	3	4
14	Sets a positive example in word and deed	O	1	2	3	4
15	*Other competencies?*	O	1	2	3	4
		O	1	2	3	4
		O	1	2	3	4

RATING INSTRUMENT FOR MENTEES

Directions: Use this tool to rate yourself on the competencies essential for being a mentee. For each competency listed in the left column, rate yourself in the right column. Use this scale: **0 = Not appropriate; 1 = Needs improvement; 2 = Able to demonstrate competency; 3 = Able to demonstrate the competency adequately; 4 = Able to demonstrate the competency very well.** When you are finished, use this tool to plan professional development to improve your mentoring competence.

Mentee Competencies		Ratings				
1	Ability to establish and maintain interpersonal rapport with others	0	1	2	3	4
2	Willingness to be mentored	0	1	2	3	4
3	Willingness to take advice	0	1	2	3	4
4	Questioning skills	0	1	2	3	4
5	Active listening skills	0	1	2	3	4
6	Self-confidence and self-efficacy	0	1	2	3	4
7	Note-taking and memory skills	0	1	2	3	4
8	Sense of humor	0	1	2	3	4
9	*Any other competencies that you can think of or that your organization wishes to add?*	0	1	2	3	4
		0	1	2	3	4
		0	1	2	3	4

GETTING STARTED IN LAUNCHING AN ORGANIZATIONAL MENTORING PROGRAM

Many organizational leaders think about launching an organizational mentoring program. Sometimes those programs are implemented to bolster classroom or online learning/training programs; sometimes they are implemented to support a talent management program; and sometimes they are implemented as stand-alone efforts to encourage leaders to take more active, hands-on roles in developing the promising people of the organization.

Even though this book is more about what mentors should do and not what organizations or mentees should do, this question is sometimes asked: *How does an organization launch a mentoring program?* Consider the following list of questions:

- What is the business need or needs that a mentoring program is intended to meet, and how will the mentoring program align with the organization's strategic business plan?
- What specific, measurable goals should the mentoring program strive to achieve?
- What roles should be played by all key stakeholders in the mentoring program? More specifically, what should be the

role of senior leaders in supporting the program? What should be the role of the HR department? What should be the roles of mentor(s) and mentees?

- Who should serve as mentors? Mentees? What qualifications or criteria should they meet?
- What should mentors and mentees do? Should the mentoring program be *formal* (in which the HR department plays match-maker to identify people to match up) or *informal* (in which the HR department trains both mentors and mentees what to do but leaves it up to mentees to take initiative to seek out their own mentors)?
- When should the mentoring process begin? Should there be some organizational cycle (such as an annual kickoff), or should it depend on the identification of individuals as High Potentials during annual talent review meetings held by the senior executives or other managers in the organization?
- Where should the mentoring process be held? Should it be encouraged on the job (in company offices or cafeteria), off the job (in restaurants or other places—even the homes of mentees or mentors), virtually (by computer or other virtual methods), or some combination? Should an effort be made to establish cross-cultural mentoring relationships in which mentor and mentee never meet face-to-face but only by computer-based meetings over Skype or similar methods?
- Why is the mentoring program being established? Are the goals clear and measurable so that results may be tracked?
- How will mentoring be done?
- How much is the organization willing to invest in the program?

By answering these questions, organizational leaders will establish a strategic framework for an effective mentoring program.

CASE STUDIES ON MENTORING*

As you read through the following case studies, underline or highlight points that evoke a reaction/emotion or remind you of an experience of your own. A series of questions follows both case studies. These can be used to guide independent reflection or to facilitate group discussion of the case studies. If reviewing the case studies as a group, consider sharing initial reactions before discussing the questions. You may also wish to consider asking group members if they are comfortable sharing their own experiences with mentorship as well. Each case study will require approximately 90 minutes to discuss, depending on the size of your group.

Case Study 1: Jane and Josie

Read the case study and answer the questions that follow it.

In the first month as a new assistant professor, Jane met many of the other faculty in the department and found two others who shared her interest in global health. One in particular, Josie, seemed willing to

---

*This Appendix is taken verbatim from K. Plamondon & CCGHR Capacity Building Task Group: Subgroup on Mentorship. (2007). *Module four: Case studies in mentorship*. Ottawa: Canadian Coalition for Global Health Research. It does not bear a copyright mark and is available for download at http://www.ccghr.ca/docs/Mentoring_Modules/Mentoring _Module4_e.pdf.

"show her the ropes" and help connect her with other people working in the University of Canada and across the country in global health research (GHR).

Josie invited Jane to attend a meeting of a group of students and faculty who were working together to build opportunities and strengthen skills in GHR on campus. The group was larger than Jane thought it would be—there were so many people working in GHR!

Josie continued to provide counsel, encouragement, and support to Jane over the next year, especially in issues related to teaching, ethics, research methodology, and the politics and policies of the University of Canada. Jane's involvement in GHR both locally and nationally grew as she found more and more opportunities to network and attend national conferences and specialized training events—much of which was facilitated directly or indirectly by Josie. Josie enjoyed the interactions with Jane and felt that she too was learning, particularly when Jane brought challenging questions forward. Josie was contemplating how she could incorporate Jane into a large program of research that had been developing over the last three years. At the end of the academic year, Jane was nominated for consideration for a new faculty award. Jane was thrilled and considered the award an encouraging sign of her future promise. When she received the award a month later, her acceptance column in the campus-wide e-mail announcement spoke of her own determination and hard work as a new faculty member on her own in an unfamiliar setting. She didn't mention the support she received from Josie. Josie had been hurt by Jane's lack of acknowledgment for her support, but wondered if she was being petty and had decided not to confront Jane about it.

Over the next two years, Jane continued to go to Josie for questions and sometimes just to "vent" about something that was frustrating her. She often asked for Josie's advice about what to do, how best to proceed, or what advice she should give to the students she was supervising. Josie sometimes felt drained by the interaction and even felt her stomach sink when Jane would knock at her door. She kept her door closed most of the time now—a major change after fifteen years of a well-known "open door" policy she held with her students. Josie didn't know what to do about it though. She thought she was making a big deal out of nothing, but didn't have anyone to talk to about it because she was worried it might be considered unprofessional to speak of a colleague in a negative way.

A month later, at Josie's promotion evaluation meeting, she was disappointed to learn that the department was divided about whether she met the promotion requirements or not. Thinking she had more than met the standards for promotion, Josie asked what concerns the department had about her qualifications or productivity over the last four years. The department replied that it wasn't to do with either. Instead, the concerns were over one of the confidential peer evaluations included in her application for promotion. The evaluation brought up concerns over Josie's ethical conduct that the department had to consider.

Josie was shocked to learn this. She immediately followed up with the two peer evaluators she'd asked months ago. Both long-term colleagues and supporters willingly shared their evaluations with Josie, neither of which revealed anything that could be considered less than forthright praise and admiration.

Josie attempted to contact Jane, but Jane did not reply to her messages. After following procedures to have the content of the third evaluation released to her, Josie learned that Jane had accused Josie of plagiarism. Jane said that Josie consistently "pumped her for ideas" and "used these for her own benefit." Josie felt betrayed, angry and violated—how could someone she supported so freely and willingly behave in such a dishonest way?

Josie began to question her own motives and interests in supporting new faculty. She thought over her interactions with Jane and wished she'd kept some notes to refer back to. After months of deliberation, Josie was able to demonstrate that the peer evaluation was not completed with her beneficence in mind and eventually received her promotion. Josie never engaged in mentoring a new faculty member again.

Questions

1. What kind of mentoring relationship is reflected in the case study?
2. What alternative approaches to mentoring can be identified?
3. What went right in this mentoring relationship?
4. What went wrong in this mentoring relationship?
5. What relational elements influencing a mentoring relationship are reflected in this case?
6. As a mentee, how would you have responded to an award nomination such as Jane received?
7. As a mentor, how would you have responded to the feelings of discomfort expressed by Josie after Jane won the award?
8. What about the nature of Jane and Josie's mentoring relationship contributed to the situation Josie found herself in during her promotional review? How could this situation have been changed?
9. How would you respond to the situation Josie found herself in during her promotional review?
10. What institutional or environmental supports were (a) available and (b) missing for both Josie and Jane in this situation?
11. What administrative strategies and individual strategies could have been used to avoid Josie's loss of interest in mentoring?

Case Study 2: Abhey

Read the case study and answer the questions that follow it.

Abhey was looking forward to his first week as a master's student. He'd worked hard for the last year to find a project, supervisor, and funding. He'd finished his undergraduate medical training a few years ago and had chosen to work in public health. After three years struggling with health policy development, he returned to university to learn, build skills and knowledge, and find out how to influence policy making in a positive way. He'd decided to focus on health policy development, hoping that he'd be able to develop some skills in influencing the health policy agenda. He had been fortunate to receive a two-year fellowship from the Health Policy Leadership (HPL) Program, which included a scholarship, special training and courses, and a mentoring program with faculty experienced in health policy.

In the first two weeks of his program, Abhey was invited to a meeting with his assigned mentor from the HPL program. These meetings were scheduled into Abhey's academic schedule every four months for one hour each time. His mentor, Aleda, had been assigned to Abhey based on the alignment of research interests, including the countries in which Abhey wished to do his research. During that first meeting, Abhey and Aleda discussed his first impressions of the program and the return to university in general. Aleda helped Abhey to identify specific goals he had for his master's program, the HPL program, and the mentoring relationship. They mutually agreed upon two of the goals to focus the mentoring on and developed a plan of action for the next four months.

Over the next year, Abhey's schedule filled up quickly and the mentoring meetings seemed to come with little time to complete the tasks and readings that Aleda would identify as helpful resources. The meetings felt a little rushed too. They were always productive and positive, but Abhey felt like they never had as much time to talk about some of the more philosophical and ethical questions being raised through his experiences in the HPL fellowship and his coursework. As his coursework came to an end and Abhey began to immerse himself more deeply in his thesis, he found the meetings to be more engaging, informal, and less rushed. They started to spend more time discussing challenges and issues related to research, ethics, and health policy. Aleda began to share more of her own personal experiences in health policy advocacy.

After two years in the HPL program, Abhey moved into a PhD after Aleda offered to incorporate him into a multi-institutional research program involving six universities, four ministries of health, and three international nongovernmental organizations across the Americas. The research team was large and involved health policy analysts, academics, health workers, and policy makers. Through the network offered by this research program, Abhey met six other doctoral students who were part of the team. Each of these students was working to strengthen health policy in resource-limited settings. As they got to know each other and began sharing ideas and experiences, the group of doctoral students discovered they all were lacking knowledge and experience in global economic policy and its interplay with health. They identified specific topics as a group, dividing the topics amongst each other for further investigation.

At the next week-long research team meeting several months later, the students organized a series of peer-learning workshops in the evenings. The six students co-facilitated the workshops using the resources, materials, and knowledge that each student had investigated. They were surprised when many of the other team members asked to join their workshops. At the end of the week, the group decided to use part of the research team's shared web space to continue their discussions. The group chose to keep the topic of global economic policy open and add other topics of interest as they emerged. Within a short period of time, members from many of the nongovernmental organizations, ministries of health, and other institutions were accessing the site and joining in the discussions. Sometimes, two or three people would identify a key interest topic and pursue it in a manner similar to how the doctoral students had done with global economic policy.

The research team considered the innovation of the six doctoral students an excellent idea and was very supportive. Several experienced researchers and policy analysts agreed to be active participants in the online discussions and began sharing their knowledge in a new way. Over the next three years, the research team joined in identifying areas of interest for building new knowledge and skills. As Abhey reflected on the evolution of the shared web space and his academic career, he felt the experience of the research team was worth sharing. Abhey approached Aleda with the idea of writing a paper on the group's experience.

Aleda loved the idea and together they brought it to the research team for consideration. True to the team environment of co-learning, the paper was published by the research team in an open-access journal the next year with plans for a series of modules on team learning and co-mentorship listed among the research team's goals for the following year.

Questions

1. What kind of mentoring relationships are reflected in the case study?
2. What alternative approaches to mentoring can be identified?
3. What about the mentoring relationships in this case facilitated positive growth for both the mentor and mentee?
4. What about the mentoring relationship contributed to expansion of the mentoring to other contexts?
5. What qualities of a good mentor are reflected by Aleda?
6. What qualities of a good mentee are reflected in Abhey?
7. Are there aspects of the shared web space that distinguish it from other types of teaching-learning interactions? What could be done to facilitate mentorship in this setting?
8. What about the nature of Abhey and Aleda's mentoring relationship contributed to the transition from formal mentoring to informal mentoring?
9. What kinds of capacity building are demonstrated in this case?
10. How is sustainability fostered by the informal mentoring that emerges later in the case study?
11. What environmental or cultural supports could be offered by the research team to ensure sustainability?

RESOURCES

This resource section is not intended to be exhaustive; rather, it presents selective resources of value. A listing here does not mean endorsement.

Johnson, R. (2005). The five steps to coaching & mentoring success. See http://ezinearticles.com/?The-Five-Steps-to-Coaching-and -Mentoring-Success&id=85418.

Lanier, J. (2010). The leadership waltz: Mentoring vs. disciplining between leaders and followers. See http://ezinearticles.com/?The -Leadership-Waltz:-Mentoring-Vs.-Discipling-Between-Leaders-and -Followers&id=5540683.

Smith, G. (2010). Effective mentoring program for leadership development. See http://ezinearticles.com/?Effective-Mentoring -Program-For-Leadership-Development&id=4731897.

Zimmerman, J. (2010). Managerial coaching and mentoring skills. See http://ezinearticles.com/?Managerial-Coaching-and-Mentoring -Skills&id=5581316.

Rockoff, J. (2008). Does mentoring reduce turnover and improve skills of new employees? Evidence from teachers in New York City. See http://papers.ssrn.com/sol3/papers.cfm?abstract_id=1147662.

Books

Maxwell, J. *Mentoring 101*. Nashville, TN: Thomas Nelson, 2008.

Stoddard, D., and R. Tamasy. *The heart of mentoring: Ten proven principles for developing people to their fullest potential*. Colorado Springs, CO: NavPress, 2009.

Zachary, L. *The mentor's guide: Facilitating effective learning relationships*. San Francisco: Jossey-Bass, 2000.

Zachary, L. *The mentee's guide: Making mentoring work for you*. San Francisco: Jossey-Bass, 2000.

Software

See http://chronus.com/products?_kk=mentoring%20program&_kt=5e276d8b-8c96-4f60-a7a4-58e319aec362&gclid=CJS_8vzViKo CFQw75Qod3gkF0g
   Description: Software to set up and administer a mentoring program in an organization

See http://www.insala.com/mentoring-programs.asp
   Description: Software to set up and administer various types of mentoring programs

See: http://www.mentoringsoftware.com/c/campaign_template
   Description: Software to facilitate online mentoring programs

Note: A web search will uncover many comparable software programs.

Videos

Jack Welch on mentoring. See http://www.youtube.com/watch?v=0ipNo1BLeIk.
   Description: A video (1:50 min.) from Jack Welch in which he describes the value of mentoring.

What is mentoring? See http://www.youtube.com/watch?v=6TTHu7
u1osk&feature=related.

Description: A video (5:47 min.) that describes the value of
mentoring.

Note: A YouTube search will uncover many useful videos on
mentoring.

REFERENCES

Allen, T. D., L. M. Finkelstein, and M. L. Poteet. *Designing Workplace Mentoring Programs: An Evidence-Based Approach*. West Sussex: Wiley-Blackwell, 2009.

Allen, T. D., E. Lentz, and R. Day. "Career Success Outcomes Associated with Mentoring Others: A Comparison of Mentors and Nonmentors." *Journal of Career Development* 32.3 (2006): 272–285.

Allen, T. D. and K. E. O'Brien. "Formal Mentoring Programs and Organizational Attraction." *Human Resource Development Quarterly* 17.1 (2006): 43–58.

Bozeman, B. and M. K. Feeney. "Toward a Useful Theory of Mentoring: A Conceptual Analysis and Critique." *Administration and Society* 39.6 (2007): 719–739.

Clark, E. "Around the Corporate Campfire: The Power of Storytelling at Work." *Reader's Digest*, Asian ed. (September 2007): 50–55.

Collins, J. and J. I. Porras. *Built to Last: Successful Habits of Visionary Companies*. New York: Collins, 2002.

DeLong, T. J., J. J. Gabarro, and R. J. Lees. "Why Mentoring Matters in a Hypercompetitive World." *Harvard Business Review* 86.1 (2008): 115–121.

Dennehy, R. F. "The Executive as Storyteller." *Management Review* 88.3 (2009): 40–43.

Denning, S. "Telling Tales." *Harvard Business Review* 82.5 (2004): 122–129.

Denning, S. "Effective Storytelling: Strategic Business Narrative Techniques." *Strategy and Leadership* 34.1 (2006): 42–48.

Denning, S. "Stories in the Workplace." *HR Magazine* 53.9 (2008): 129–132.

Ensher, E. A. and S. E. Murphy. *Power Mentoring: How Successful Mentors and Protégés Get the Most Out of Their Relationships.* San Francisco: Jossey-Bass, 2005.

Fowler, J. L. and J. G. O'Gorman. "Mentoring Functions: A Contemporary View of the Perceptions of Mentees and Mentors." *British Journal of Management* 16.1 (2005): 51–57.

Garvey, B. "The Mentoring/Counseling/Coaching Debate." *Development and Learning in Organizations* 18.2 (2004): 6–8.

Goleman, D. and R. Boyatzis. "Social Intelligence and the Biology of Leadership." *Harvard Business Review* 86.9 (2008): 74–81.

Hagel, J., J. S. Brown, and L. Davison. "Talent Is Everything." *The Conference Board Review* 46.3 (2009): 24–33.

Harris, J. and B. K. Barnes. "Leadership Storytelling." *Industrial and Commercial Training* 38.7 (2006): 350–353.

Heath, C. and D. Heath. *Made to Stick: Why Some Ideas Take Hold and Others Come Unstuck.* London: Random House Books, 2007.

Ives, Y. "What Is 'Coaching'? An Exploration of Conflicting Paradigms." *International Journal of Evidence Based Coaching and Mentoring* 6.2 (2008): 100–113.

Liang, B., R. Spencer, D. Brogan, and M. Corral. "Mentoring Relationships from Early Adolescence Through Emerging Adulthood: A Qualitative Analysis." *Journal of Vocational Behavior* 72.2 (2008): 168–182.

Maxwell, R. and R. Dickman. *The Elements of Persuasion*. New York: Collins, 2007.

Murrell, A. J., S. Forte-Trammell, and D. A. Bing. *Intelligent Mentoring: How IBM Creates Value Through People, Knowledge, and Relationships*. Upper Saddle River, NJ: IBM Press, 2009.

"New guard: Denise Lee." *T+D* 59.9: 104.

Pink, D. H. *A Whole New Mind: Why Right-Brainers Will Rule the Future*. New York: Riverhead Books, 2006.

Rothwell, W. *Invaluable Knowledge: Securing Your Company's Technical Expertise—Recruiting and Retaining Top Talent, Transferring Technical Knowledge, Engaging High Performers*. New York: Amacom, 2011.

Scandura, T. A. and R. E. Viator. "Mentoring in Public Accounting Firms: An Analysis of Mentor-Protégé Relationships, Mentorship Functions, and Protégé Turnover Intentions." *Accounting, Organizations and Society* 19.8 (1994): 717–734.

Shaw, G., R. Brown, and P. Bromiley. "Strategic Stories: How 3M Is Rewriting Business Planning." *Harvard Business Review* 76.3 (1998): 41–50.

INDEX

Note: page numbers in *italics* refer to exhibits

ABOUT THE AUTHORS

William J. Rothwell, Ph.D., SPHR, is president of Rothwell & Associates, Inc. (see www.rothwell-associates.com), a full-service consulting company. He is also Professor of Workforce Education and Development in the Department of Learning and Performance Systems on the University Park campus of The Pennsylvania State University. He leads a graduate emphasis program in workplace learning and performance that has consistently been listed over the past decade among the top ten best graduate programs in *U.S. News and World Report*. He had 20 years of full-time work experience in human resources in both government and business before becoming a consultant and university professor in 1993.

Best-known for his extensive and high-profile consulting work in succession planning and talent management with hundreds of organizations in the United States and around the world, Rothwell is a frequent speaker or keynoter at conferences and seminars around the world. In 2012, he was presented the American Society for Training and Development's (ASTD) prestigious Distinguished Contribution to Workplace Learning and Performance Award; in 2004, he earned the Graduate Faculty Teaching Award at Pennsylvania State University, a single award given each year to the best graduate faculty member on the 24 campuses of the Penn State University system. His train-the-trainer programs have received global recognition and awards for excellence from Motorola University and from Linkage, Inc. He has authored, coauthored, edited, or coedited more than 300 books, book chapters, and articles—including 80 books (at current count).

Dr. Rothwell has been very active in the American Society of Training and Development (ASTD), serving in numerous capacities, including chair of the Publishing Review Committee for several years, chapter president for two ASTD local Chapters, and membership on the ASTD National Awards Committee, the ASTD Dissertation Awards Committee, and the ASTD Research Article of the Year Committee. He also acted as chief investigator for research on five ASTD competency studies, including the most recent one in 2012. His recent books include *Talent Management: An Action-Oriented Step-by-Step Approach* (2012); the edited three-volume *Encyclopedia of Human Resource Management* (2012); *Lean But Agile: Rethink Workforce Planning and Gain a True Competitive Advantage* (2012); *Invaluable Knowledge* (2011); *Competency-Based Training Basics* (2010); *Effective Succession Planning: Ensuring Leadership Continuity and Building Talent from Within*, 4th ed. (2010); *Practicing Organization Development*, 3rd ed. (2009); *The Manager's Guide to Maximizing Employee Potential: Quick and Easy Ways to Build Talent Every Day* (2009); *Basics of Adult Learning* (2009); *HR Transformation: Demonstrating Strategic Leadership in the Face of Future Trends* (2008); and *Working Longer: New Strategies for Managing, Training, and Retaining Older Employees* (2008).

His older books include *Cases in Linking Workforce Development to Economic Development: Community College Partnering for Training, Individual Career Planning, and Community and Economic Development* (2008); *Human Performance Improvement: Building Practitioner Performance* (2007); *Instructor Excellence: Mastering the Delivery of Training* (2007); *Next Generation Management Development: The Complete Guide and Resource* (2007); *Handbook of Training Technology: An Introductory Guide to Facilitating Learning with Technology—From Planning Through Evaluation* (2006); *Beyond Training and Development: The Groundbreaking Classic on Human Performance Enhancement* (2005); *Mapping the Future: Shaping New Workplace Learning and Performance Competencies* (2004); *Improving On-the-Job Training: How to Establish and Operate a Comprehensive OJT Program* (2004); *Linking Training to Performance: A Guide for Workforce Developers* (2004); *Competency-Based Human*

Resource Management (2004); *The Strategic Development of Talent* (2003); *What CEOs Expect from Corporate Training: Building Workplace Learning and Performance Initiatives That Advance Organizational Goals* (2003); *Planning and Managing Human Resources: Strategic Planning for Human Resource Management* (2003)l; *Creating In-House Sales Training and Development Programs: A Competency-Based Approach to Building Sales Ability* (2002); *The Workplace Learner: How to Align Training Initiatives with Individual Learning Competencies* (2002); *Building Effective Technical Training: How to Develop Hard Skills in Organizations* (2002); *The ASTD Reference Guide to Workplace Learning and Performance: Present and Future Roles,* 3rd ed. (2000); *The Complete Guide to Training Delivery: A Competency-Based Approach* (2000); *ASTD Models for Human Performance: Roles, Competencies, Outputs,* 2nd ed. (2000); *The Competency Toolkit,* 2 Vols. (2000); *The Analyst* (2000); *The Evaluator* (2000); *Developing In-House Leadership and Management Development Programs: Their Creation, Management, and Continuous Improvement* (1999); *The Action Learning Guidebook: A Real-Time Strategy for Problem-Solving, Training Design, and Employee Development* (1999); *ASTD Models for Workplace Learning and Performance: Roles, Competencies, Work Outputs* (1999); *The Sourcebook for Self-Directed Learning* (1998); *In Action: Improving Human Performance* (1998); *In Action: Linking HRD and Organizational Strategy* (1998); *Beyond Instruction: Comprehensive Program Planning for Business and Education* (1997); and *The Emerging Issues in Human Resource Development Sourcebook* (1997).

Rothwell can be reached by email at wjr9@psu.edu or by phone at 814-863-2581.

Dr. Peter Chee is president and CEO of ITD World (The Institute of Training and Development), a leading multinational corporation for Human Resource Development. With Dr. Chee's leadership contribution for more than 26 years, ITD World has established itself as a global learning solutions expert.

He works in close partnership with best-selling and award-winning author William J. Rothwell, who has written more than 80 books and Jack Canfield, the world's leading success coach and authority on peak performance who holds the Guinness Book of World Records for the most books on *New York Times* bestseller list with 210 books and 125 million copies in print. Dr. Chee and Dr. Jack Canfield are co-authors of *Coaching for Breakthrough Success* whereas Dr. Chee and Dr. William Rothwell are coauthors of the book entitled *Becoming an Effective Mentoring Leader*. Dr. Chee is also the author of *The 12 Disciplines of Leadership Excellence* with Brian Tracy.

Dr. Chee holds a Doctor of Business Administration Degree from the University of South Australia (UniSA), an MSc. in Training and HRM from the University of Leicester, UK, and was also a Graduate of the Chartered Institute of Marketing, UK. He holds a Certificate in Change Management and Performance Consulting from Pennsylvania State University, ranked the #1 university in the United States for postgraduate programs in HRD, and a Certificate in Human Performance Improvement (HPI) from The American Society of Training and Development (ASTD). Dr. Chee's doctoral research work lies in the area of motivation and performance management.

As a trainer and developer of leaders and senior executives from more than 80 countries, Dr. Chee's training, coaching, consulting, and research experience resonate in the areas of personal excellence; the success principles—techniques for breakthrough results; leadership and team excellence; coaching and mentoring excellence; work, life, and time management; motivation and performance management; strategic management; sales and marketing; human resource development; and creativity and innovation.

Dr. Chee was the creator of the Coaching Principles (TCP), the Situational Coaching Model (SCM), and Achievers Coaching

Techniques (ACT). He is a leading certified trainer for Dr. John C. Maxwell programs (the world's #1 leadership guru), Zig Ziglar programs (the world's #1 motivation guru), and a certified master trainer for Jack Canfield programs. Dr. Chee is the chief coach and developer of the Certified Coaching and Mentoring Professional (CCMP) program's Advance Certificate in Coaching and Certificate in Performance Coaching, which is accredited and recognized by the International Coaching Federation (ICF).

He is a Baden Powell Fellow of the World Scout Foundation bestowed by the King of Sweden. In the international HRD arena, Dr. Chee served as the president of ARTDO International (Asian Regional Training and Development Organisation) in 2004 and once again in 2010. ARTDO International, established in 1974, is a nonprofit professional umbrella body that brings together renowned national HRD bodies, local and multinational companies active in HRD work, and HRD professionals from more than 30 countries around the world.

He has fulfilled many of his dreams. His purpose-driven life is to transform leaders for a better world with love for God and people. He is a strong believer and practitioner of life coaching and mentoring that evokes excellence in others for greater success and happiness in work and life.

To invite Dr. Peter Chee to speak at your events or to train and coach your team, please go to www.itdworld.com/speakers.

For further information on Dr. Peter Chee and his work at ITD World, please visit: www.itdworld.com.

ABOUT THE
CONTRIBUTING AUTHORS

Colin Tan is a senior associate consultant with ITD World, a leading multinational provider of corporate training, professional competency certification, business education, and coaching and consulting services in areas relating to management, human resources, and organizational development, as well as at mega events and conferences in Asia Pacific.

Tan graduated with a degree in molecular biology and biochemistry (with honors) from Middlebury College, one of the "Little Ivies" in the United States. After graduation, he worked as a manager in Singapore, Indonesia, and Malaysia. Specifically, he was involved in branch management work at Regional Container Lines (a Thai shipping company with an operational headquarters in Singapore) in Indonesia, and later in corporate planning and business development work at MS, a Malaysian joint-venture company with Toshiba.

In 2002, he left the world of management to pursue his personal interest in research, consultancy, and training. Over the years, he has acquired extensive knowledge and expertise in human performance improvement, organizational development, and marketing research. He was deeply involved in several human performance improvement and marketing research–intensive projects in the recent past.

Tan has consulted in the area of human performance improvement, employing human performance technologies. Colin is an ARTDO International–ITD Certified Training Professional and a certified trainer for "The Laws of Teamwork," a team-building program developed by world-renowned leadership guru, Dr. John C. Maxwell.

Dr. Low Hun Seng is the director of ITD World, a leading multinational provider of corporate training, professional competency certification, business education, and coaching and consulting services in areas relating to management, human resources, and organizational development, as well as at mega events and conferences in Asia Pacific.

With 30 years of working experience, including 20 years in the banking industry as vice president at a local bank and 5 years as general manager for a training institute, he is currently the senior consultant and director at the Institute of Training and Development. He is instrumental in the development and delivery of the mentoring module for ITD World's Certified Coaching and Mentoring Professional, where he also acts as a mentor-coach to the participants.

In the past, he served in various nonprofit organizations: as chairperson for a church-based kindergarten; as advisor to MITD, and as deputy organizing chair for ARTDO International HR Event (2010) in Kuala Lumpur. Currently, he is acting as advisor to Georgetown World Heritage Trust Inc., an entity responsible for promoting, preserving, and protecting the cultural heritage of Georgetown.

Dr. Low believes in the ideal of "helping individuals and organizations to learn how to learn" as the basis of self-development and enhancing human potential. He has had the great opportunity to learn personally from many wonderful leaders and gurus including Dr. Lin See Yan, Dr. William Rothwell, Dr. John Maxwell, Tom Crane, and Jack Canfield.

He holds a Bachelor of Commerce degree from the Birmingham University; was an associate member of the Chartered Institute of Bankers, London; and earned his MBA degree from Heriot Watt University and a doctorate degree from the University of South Australia. His research emphasis resides in the domain of organizational learning and mentoring.